A GUIDE TO EMERGENCY HEALTH MANAGEMENT AFTER NATURAL DISASTER

Scientific Publication No. 407

PAN AMERICAN HEALTH ORGANIZATION
Pan American Sanitary Bureau, Regional Office of the
WORLD HEALTH ORGANIZATION
525 Twenty-third Street, N.W.
Washington, D.C. 20037, U.S.A.

1981

Issued in Spanish (1981) as:

*Administración sanitaria de emergencia
con posterioridad a los
desastres naturales*

ISBN 92 75 11407 2

Contents

PART I: THE EFFECTS OF DISASTER ON HEALTH
AND AN APPROACH TO RELIEF

PART II: EMERGENCY RELIEF PROCEDURES

PREFACE

This *Guide* is intended for use by decision makers and senior administrators in disaster-prone developing countries who are responsible for providing health services after sudden natural disasters.

It presents a general overview of the problems that will be encountered when a disaster overcomes a nation's resources and suggests general criteria that should be applied in choosing relief measures. It is not within the *Guide's* scope to elaborate on the technical aspects of the measures chosen for implementation. The Pan American Health Organization will later publish detailed technical guidelines on specialized topics such as the management of medical supplies, vector-control measures, health management in refugee camps, and communicable disease surveillance as a series of manuals.

For the purposes of this *Guide*, natural disasters comprise earthquakes, volcanic eruptions, floods, tidal waves, and destructive winds (cyclones, hurricanes, and tornadoes). Man-made catastrophes, famine, drought, and other slow-onset disasters, and epidemics are not included. The *Guide's* object is not to give detailed technical information but to present a framework within which an administrator can make rational and effective decisions about relief measures. It deals only with the period immediately after disaster—the first three or four weeks—and not with long-term problems of reconstruction and rehabilitation. Nor is it intended to anticipate every circumstance; to meet local conditions, some adaptation of the approaches suggested will be necessary. It is hoped the *Guide* will serve as a framework for developing national manuals covering local circumstances. It should be emphasized that the health sector must work within the framework and priorities that higher levels of authority establish during this period, and that greater priority may be given to other sectors.

The *Guide* is divided into two sections. The first presents a summary of experience with common public health problems after natural disasters. The second and longer part deals with specific health topics and relief procedures.

ACKNOWLEDGMENT AND REFERENCES

This publication has been made possible by the competent and dedicated contribution of Dr. John Seaman, Senior Medical Officer, Save the Children Fund, London, who drafted and reviewed its preliminary versions.

Acknowledgment is owed many people in and outside the World Health Organization for their valuable comments and criticism based on long field experience. We are particularly grateful to UNICEF, the U.S. Centers for Disease Control, the League of Red Cross Societies and the American Red Cross, the Research Center on Disaster Epidemiology in Belgium, and the many individual experts in disaster-prone countries who contributed their comments to the extensive revision of several chapters. Thanks are also due Dr. Claude de Ville de Goyet and Mr. David Donaldson of the Pan American Health Organization and Dr. Wolfgang Bulle of the U.S. Centers for Disease Control for their detailed technical review of the drafts and preparation of the manuscript.

The valuable contributions and comments from all World Health Organization regions and especially WHO's Emergency Relief Operations Office in Geneva have made it possible to address the problem globally.

Material and ideas have been drawn from many sources, but particularly from the following publications which are essential complements to this Guide:

1. de Ville de Goyet, C., J. Seaman, and U. Geiger. *The Management of Nutritional Emergencies in Large Populations.* Geneva, World Health Organization, 1978.

2. *The Selection of Essential Drugs; Report of a WHO Expert Committee.* Geneva, World Health Organization, 1979. (WHO Technical Report Series 641.)

3. Protein-Calorie Advisory Group of the United Nations System. *A Guide to Food and Health Relief Operations for Disasters.* New York, United Nations, 1977.

4. Assar, M. *A Guide to Sanitation in Natural Disasters.* Geneva, World Health Organization, 1971.

Additional reading materials are listed in Annex 2.

Part I

**THE EFFECTS OF DISASTER
ON HEALTH AND AN
APPROACH TO RELIEF**

AN OVERVIEW

Sudden natural disasters are often believed to cause not only widespread death but also massive social disruption and outbreaks of epidemic disease and famine which leave survivors entirely dependent on outside relief. Systematic observation of the effects of disaster on human health has led to rather different conclusions, both about the effects of disaster on health and about the most effective ways of providing relief. Though all disasters are unique in that they affect areas with differing social, medical, and economic backgrounds, there are still similarities between disasters which, if recognized, can optimize the management of health relief and use of resources (see Table 1). The following points may be noted:

(1) There is a relationship between the type of disaster and its effect on health. This is particularly true of the immediate impact in causing injuries: earthquakes regularly cause many injuries requiring medical care, while floods and tidal waves cause relatively few.

(2) Some effects are a potential rather than an inevitable threat to health. For example, population movement and other environmental changes may lead to increased risk of disease transmission, although epidemics generally do not result from disasters.

(3) The actual and potential health risks after disaster do not all occur at the same time. Instead, they tend to arise at different times and to vary in importance within a disaster-affected area. Thus, casualties occur mainly at the time and place of im-

Table 1. Short-term effects of major natural disaster.

Effect	Earthquakes	High winds (without floodings)	Tidal waves/ flash flood	Floods
Deaths	Many	Few	Many	Few
Severe injuries requiring extensive care	Overwhelming	Moderate	Few	Few
Increased risk of communicable diseases	Potential risk following all major disasters (Probability rising with overcrowding and deteriorating sanitation)			
Food scarcity	Rare	Rare (may occur due to factors other than food shortage)	Common	Common
Major population movements	Rare	Rare (may occur in heavily damaged urban areas)	Common	Common

pact and require immediate medical care, while the risks of increased disease transmission take longer to develop and are greatest where there is crowding and standards of sanitation have declined.

(4) Disaster-created needs for food, shelter, and primary health care are usually not total. Even displaced persons often salvage some of the basic necessities of life. Further, people generally recover quickly from their immediate shock and spontaneously engage in search and rescue, transport of the injured, and other private relief activities.

Effective health relief management hence depends on anticipating and as they arise identifying problems and delivering specific materials at the precise times and points where they are needed. The ability to transport maximum supplies and personnel to a disaster area is much less essential.

Health Problems Common to All Disasters

Social Reactions

Behavior after a major disaster is only rarely generalized panic or stunned waiting. Spontaneous yet highly organized individual action occurs as survivors rapidly recover from their initial shock and set about purposefully achieving clear ends. Earthquake survivors often begin search and rescue activities minutes after an impact and within hours may have organized themselves in groups to transport the injured to medical posts. Actively antisocial behavior such as widespread looting occurs only in exceptional circumstances.

Although everyone thinks his spontaneous reactions are entirely rational, they may be detrimental to the community's higher interests. A person's conflicting roles as family head and health official, for instance, have in some instances resulted in key relief people not reporting to duty until their relatives and property are safe.

Rumors abound, particularly of epidemics. As a result, considerable pressure may be put on the authorities to undertake relief work such as mass vaccination against typhoid or cholera for which there is no sound technical reason. In addition, people may be reluctant to submit to relief measures which the authorities think necessary. After earthquakes or before predicted floods, for example, people are reluctant to evacuate even if their homes have been or are likely to be completely destroyed.

These patterns of behavior have two major implications for those making decisions about relief programs. First, patterns of behavior and demands for relief can be limited and modified by keeping the population informed and by obtaining necessary information before embarking on extended relief programs. Second, the population itself will provide most rescue and first aid, take the injured to hospitals if they are accessible, build temporary shelters, and carry out other essential tasks. Additional resources should therefore be directed toward meeting needs survivors themselves cannot meet.

Communicable Disease

Disaster does not usually result in outbreaks of infectious diseases, although in certain circumstances it does increase the potential for disease transmission. The most frequently observed increases in disease are caused by fecal contamination of water and food; hence, such diseases are mainly enteric.

The risk of epidemic communicable diseases is proportional to population density and displacement, which increases the load on water and food and its risk of contamination, as in refugee camps, disruption of preexisting sanitary services such as piped water and sewerage, and failure to maintain or restore normal public health programs in the immediate postdisaster period.

In the longer run, an increase in vector-borne diseases may occur in some areas because of disruption of vector control efforts. Residual insecticides may be washed away from buildings and the number of mosquito breeding sites may increase. As an example, 75,000 cases of malaria occurred in Haiti in the five months following the October 3-4, 1963, hurricane there.

Population Displacements

When large spontaneous or organized population movements occur, an urgent need to provide relief is created. People may move to urban areas where public services cannot cope, and the result may be an increase in morbidity and mortality. Thus, 6,000 excess deaths occurred in Dacca, Bangladesh, after floods there in 1974. If much housing has been destroyed, large population movements may occur within urban areas as people seek shelter with relatives and friends. Surveys of settlements and towns around Managua following the December 23, 1972, earthquake in Nicaragua indicated that 80 to 90 per cent of the 200,000 people displaced were living with relatives and friends, 5 to 10 per cent were living in parks, city squares, and vacant lots, and the remainder were living in schools and other buildings.

Climatic Exposure

The health hazards of exposure to the elements are small, even after disasters in cold countries. As long as the population is dry, reasonably well clothed, and able to find windbreaks, death from exposure does not appear to be a major risk. The need to provide emergency shelter therefore varies greatly with local conditions; it may be needed for other reasons.

Food and Nutrition

Food shortages in the immediate aftermath may arise in two ways. Food stock destruction within the disaster area may reduce the absolute amount of food available, or disruption of distribution systems may curtail access to food even if there is no absolute shortage. Generalized food shortages severe enough to cause nutritional problems do not occur after earthquakes.

Flooding and sea surges often damage household food stocks and crops, disrupt distribution, and cause major local shortages. Food distribution, at least in the short term, is often a major and urgent need, but large-scale distribution is not always necessary.

Mental Health

Anxiety, neuroses, and depression are not major, acute public health problems following disasters, and family and neighbors can deal with them temporarily. Wherever possible, efforts should be made to preserve family and community social structures. The indiscriminate use of sedatives and tranquilizers during the emergency relief phase is strongly discouraged. In developed countries, mental health problems are reported to be significant during long-term rehabilitation and reconstruction and may need to be dealt with during that phase.

Health Problems Related to the Type of Disaster

Earthquakes

Usually because of dwelling destruction, earthquakes may cause many deaths (more than 10 per cent of the population) and injure large numbers of people. The toll depends mostly on three factors.

The first is housing type. Houses built of adobe or dry stone, even if only a single story high, are highly unstable and their collapse causes many deaths and injuries. Lighter forms of construction, especially wood-framing, have proved much less dangerous. After the 1976 earthquake in Guatemala, for example, a survey showed that in one village with a population of 1,577, all those killed (78) and severely injured had been in adobe buildings, whereas all residents of woodframe buildings survived. The second is the time of day at which the earthquake occurs. The last is population density, for the total number of deaths and injuries is likely to be much higher in densely populated areas.

The ratio of dead to injured after earthquakes has been found to be approximately 1 to 3 when they result from the primary shock.

There are large variations within disaster-affected areas. Mortalities of up to 85 per cent occasionally occur in towns close to an earthquake's epicenter. As an example, the September 1978 earthquake at Tabas-e-Golshan, Iran, killed 11,000 of the town's 13,000 residents. The ratio of dead to injured decreases as the distance from the epicenter increases. Some age groups are more affected than others, for fit adults are spared more than small children and the old, who are less able to protect themselves.

Secondary disaster may occur after earthquakes and increase the number of casualties requiring medical attention. Historically, the greatest risk is from fire, although in recent decades postearthquake fires causing mass casualties have been uncommon.

Little information is available about the kinds of injuries resulting from earthquakes, but regardless of the number of casualties, the broad pattern of injury is likely to be a mass of injured with minor cuts and bruises, a smaller group suffering from simple fractures, and another group with serious multiple fractures or internal injuries requiring surgery and other intensive treatment. After the 1968 earthquake south of Khorasan, Iran, for example, only 368 (3.3 per cent) of 11,254 people treated by emergency services (including some routine medical cases) required inpatient care.

Most demand for health services occurs within the first 24 hours. Injured people may appear at medical facilities only during the first three to five days, after which presentation patterns return almost to normal. A good example of the crucial importance of the timing of emergency care is seen in the number of admissions to a field hospital after the 1976 earthquake in Guatemala shown in Figure 1. From day 6

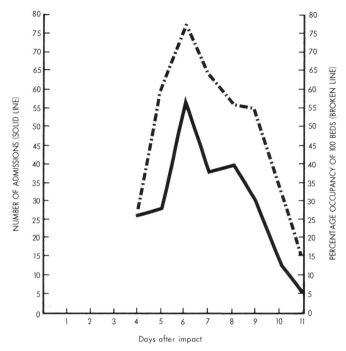

Figure 1. Admissions and occupancy rates at the field hospital in Chimaltenango, Guatemala, 1976.

onward, admissions fell dramatically despite intensive casefinding in remote rural areas.

Patients may appear in two waves, the first consisting of casualties from the immediate area around the medical facility and the second of referrals as relief operations in more distant areas become organized.

Destructive Winds

Unless they are complicated by secondary disasters such as the floods or sea surges often associated with them, destructive winds cause relatively few deaths and injuries. As an example, the major cyclone that in 1974 destroyed much of Darwin, Australia, a town of 45,000, caused only 51 deaths and led to a total of 145 hospital admissions, of which 110 were for severe lacerations and other relatively moderate

7

trauma. Effective warning before such windstorms will limit morbidity and mortality, and most injuries will be relatively trivial.

Flash Floods and Sea Surges

These may cause much death but leave relatively few severely injured in their wake. Deaths result mainly from drowning and are commonest among the weakest members of the population. Thus, the November 1977 cyclone/sea surge disaster that affected a population of 700,000 in Andhra Pradesh, India, killed at least 10,000 people but left only 177 orthopedic cases (mostly arm and leg fractures) that required evacuation.

Floods

Slow flooding causes limited immediate morbidity and mortality. A slight increase in deaths from venomous snake bites has been reported but not fully substantiated, and traumatic injuries caused by flooding require only limited health care.

Part II

**EMERGENCY RELIEF
PROCEDURES**

Chapter 1

COORDINATION OF NATIONAL RELIEF ACTIVITIES AND ASSESSMENT OF HEALTH NEEDS

National Emergency Committee

After a natural disaster, all resources of the affected country are mobilized. Often they are placed under the direction of a single national authority in accordance with emergency legislation adopted beforehand.

An emergency committee or a civil defense agency generally attached to the presidency or defense or interior ministry will assume the overall coordination and sometimes command of emergency activities related to health.

The emergency committee is likely to be organized as shown in Figure 2. Each country's organization will reflect its specific administrative, social, and political structure. Final responsibility for equipment such as heavy vehicles and telecommunications and authority to request or accept external assistance and issue news releases on health matters will probably lie outside the health sector.

Health Relief Coordinator

Within the health sector, the establishment of a single focal point for coordination is essential to ensure the optimal use of the health-care resources available to the health ministry, social security agency, armed forces, and private sector. A Health Relief Coordinator should normally be designated before a disaster as part of the country's predisaster planning. Should this step have been overlooked, a senior official must be appointed to represent the health sector within the emergency committee, direct the sector's relief activities and set its priorities, clear news releases, approve requests for external cooperation, and accept or reject offers of assistance.

Health Relief Committee

Coordination of all components—public and private—of the health sector requires that a small committee be set up to assist the Coordinator. Representatives of all major government agencies providing health care, the Red Cross, voluntary agencies, and perhaps the international community will meet periodically or continuously to advise the Coordinator and integrate their agencies' activities with the overall relief and rehabilitation effort.

Figure 3 illustrates the various functional areas that the Coordinator and the committee should consider in organizing relief operations. Several activities such as transportation, supplies, and volunteer coordination must be integrated with the corresponding areas in the national emergency committee (Figure 2). The health transportation unit, for instance, will work closely with and under the national emergency committee's transport section.

11

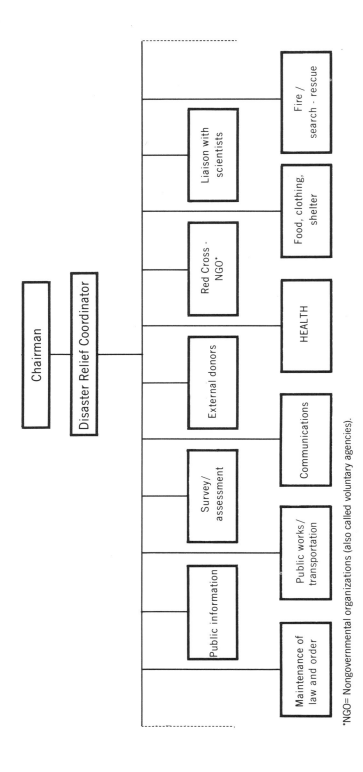

*NGO= Nongovernmental organizations (also called voluntary agencies).

Figure 2. Organization of a national emergency committee.

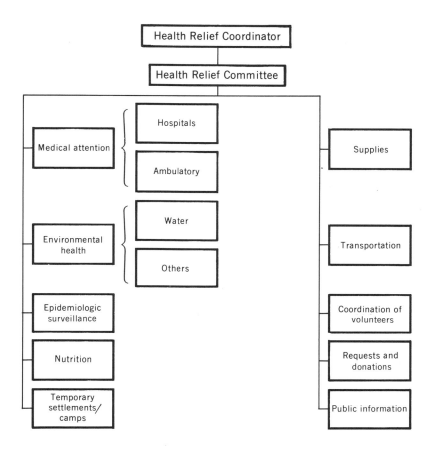

Figure 3. Coordination of health relief activities.

Assessment of Needs: Objectives

The major administrative problem in past relief operations has been a mass of conflicting and often exaggerated reports about the extent and effects of the disaster. Factual information will be required to meet three main objectives: defining the affected population, identifying and anticipating its unmet needs, which is accomplished by assessing the extent of damage and existing local human and material resources, and identifying potential secondary risks to health. The Health Relief Coordinator will also require information to keep the international relief community abreast of the changing situation in order for it to respond appropriately, provide verified facts to the national and international media in order to avoid unsubstantiated reports such as of disease outbreaks that may stimulate inappropriate responses, and keep the local population accurately informed about available services and prevent or counteract rumors.

Type of Information

Figures 4 and 5 show probable changes in needs and relief priorities at different periods after earthquakes and floods, respectively. The major information requirements for emergency relief after different types of disaster are: (1) the geographic area affected, an estimate of the population, and its location in the affected area; (2) the status of transport (rail, road, air) and communications systems; (3) the availability of potable water, food stocks, sanitary facilities, and shelter; (4) the number of casualties; (5) the status and capacity of hospitals and other health facilities in the affected area and their specific drug and personnel needs; (6) the location and numbers of people who have moved away from their homes, e.g., into urban areas or to roadsides or high ground; and (7) an estimate of the numbers of dead and missing. The last has low priority when the major concern is providing essential services to survivors.

In the first few days, provision of immediate relief and collection of information will be simultaneous activities. As urgent relief needs are met, information can be collected on specific topics to define further relief priorities.

Background Information

Collecting and interpreting information will be simplified if background information is maintained in a summary and easily accessible form (displayed, when possible, as maps) as part of a predisaster plan.

It should show the size and distribution of population in the area; major communication lines and topography; health facilities' distribution and services, with notations of those that might be particularly vulnerable to natural disasters as determined by prior engineering studies; the location of large food and medicine stocks in government stores, wholesalers' warehouses, and major voluntary and international agencies; key people and organizations currently active in relief, and the location of potential evacuation areas.

Methods of Gathering Information after the Impact

Information can be obtained in four main ways: aerial observation (light aircraft, helicopters, satellites); reports directly from the community and relief workers; regular reporting systems for specific items of information; and surveys.

Aerial Observations

If light aircraft or helicopters are available, low-altitude overflights may yield rapid information on the geographic extent of damage and major damage to bridges, roads, and other specific lines of communication. This information is of limited use in determining the operational capacity of facilities and damage to underground installations. Helicopters have great flexibility and health workers should try to use them early on in assessing needs.

Satellite and high-altitude aerial photography is of little use in providing health information in the first weeks after disaster. Although the technology of high-altitude and satellite photography is rapidly changing and becoming more flexible, it appears likely that its major application will be in predisaster planning such as flood-zone mapping and in information acquisition for long-term reconstruction.

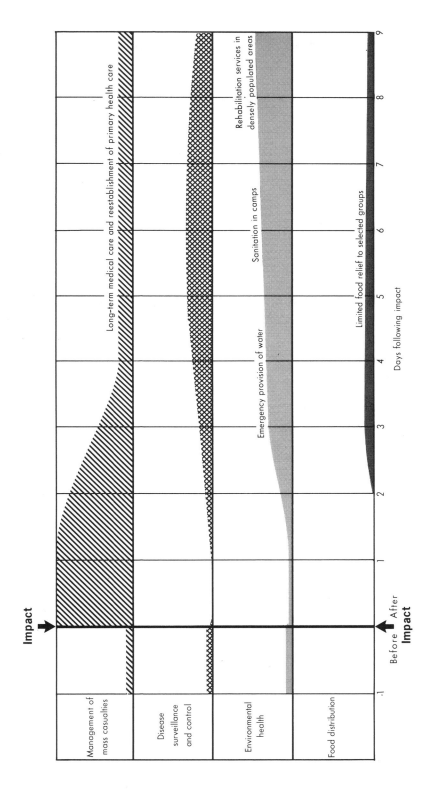

Figure 4. Changing needs and priorities following earthquakes.

15

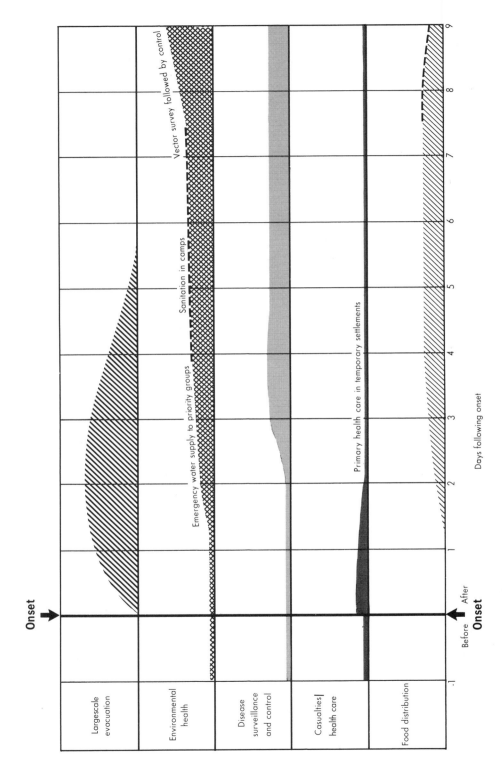

Figure 5. Changing needs and priorities following floods/sea surges.

16

Reports are received from community leaders, administrators, and local authorities, but often they contain serious shortcomings since they lack information about isolated, severely affected communities. Sometimes the respondent may have little accurate information to report and exaggerate the importance or urgency of some needs. Where reasonable doubt exists, the health relief committee should not accept requests for large-scale relief at face value, but should try to discover why a particular need is said to exist. Relief teams sent to affected communities should also be instructed to provide basic information on their health needs and ability to cope with them.

Regular Reporting from Existing Facilities

Where communications can be reestablished rapidly, information must be sought directly from administrative centers, public and private hospitals, and other technical agencies about immediate medical care, water, food, and sanitation needs.

If large numbers of casualties are expected, for instance, daily reports should begin to be gathered from major health facilities as soon as possible after the impact to establish their ability to cope with the increased load and needs for support. A standard reporting format should be used by all components of each agency (health ministry, social security agency, armed forces, voluntary agencies, private sector). The information collected should include the numbers of casualties appearing for treatment each day, other patients, admissions, vacant beds, and deaths. If possible, attendance and admissions should be reported by broad age and diagnostic categories.

Essential materials in short supply such as casting plaster or x-ray film and specific food, water, and power problems should also be reported. As noted in Chapter 3, on disease surveillance, epidemiologic techniques are particularly useful in gathering and evaluating this information.

Surveys

Objective and quantified information on certain health needs can be obtained only by systematic surveying. If existing information sources are inadequate or inaccurate, suitable surveys should be conducted as soon as possible. After a major disaster, surveys may be organized in three stages:

First, *an initial rapid survey* of need, generally aerial, delineates the affected area by examining all potentially affected areas. The physical condition of health-care, transport, and communications facilities as well as the status of relief activities should be quickly assessed. This will be sufficient to establish the types of problems that have arisen, to serve as a basis for mobilizing specific relief, and to design more formal surveys. The initial survey is generally the responsibility of the armed forces.

Familiarity with the area to be surveyed is most important. Participation by health professionals in the survey will be an asset, but is not essential as the data are not highly technical and can be gathered by others.

There is generally conflict between the need for assessing the overall problem and the need for immediate humanitarian assistance. To resolve this, surveillance personnel should be prohibited whenever possible from giving medical care and backup medical assistance must be provided.

Second, *a detailed multidisciplinary survey* must attempt to include all affected areas. Some of the following information not directly related to survival should be collected through sampling which statisticians have helped design.

During the first days, a survey in outlying areas should include an assessment of the numbers of casualties and dead. A survey of health needs must be made part of emergency care so that the survey team can call in immediate medical backup. Information should be collected on (1) the total number of casualties; (2) number requiring evacuation and their major diagnostic categories; (3) number requiring local treatment; (4) availability of essential health supplies and personnel; (5) continued aftercare likely to be needed for those receiving emergency treatment; and (6) need to supply or reconstruct local medical facilities.

The detailed survey will try to assess the immediate impact of the disaster on water quality and availability. The aim is to estimate the extent to which damage to water supply systems and other sanitary services immediately increase health hazards over predisaster conditions, not to assess their absolute quality.

The need for food, shelter, and protective clothing must also be assessed.

In contrast to the initial rapid survey, it is essential to have the most qualified available health professionals take part in this survey since major relief plans will be based on their findings. At least one survey team member should be chosen for his familiarity with local conditions. Since technical competence and prior experience in disaster assessment are major assets, however, regional or international personnel may have to be called on to provide expertise not available locally. Neighboring countries should consider pooling such resources before disasters occur on the principle of technical cooperation among developing countries.

Transporting the survey teams must be given highest priority since competition with other relief activities for available transportation will increase. Specifically, survey team space should be sought on all relief transport if the teams do not have their own transportation. Helicopters are the most flexible and useful transport for such surveying.

Third, *surveys of specific problems* must be made at the same time as other surveys. Damage to health facilities and related utilities should be surveyed throughout the affected area by competent technicians and engineers. These surveys will provide a basis for reconstruction cost estimates. If such cost estimates are not quickly available, scarce international relief funds cannot be suitably channeled to priority areas in the health sector. Finally, these surveys will start the continuing surveillance needed to direct relief activities rationally.

Chapter 2

MANAGEMENT OF MASS CASUALTIES

Medical treatment and nursing care for large numbers of casualties are likely to be needed only after certain types of disasters. Most injuries are sustained in the initial impact, and thus the greatest need for emergency care occurs in the first two days.

The burden of organizing and delivering transport, first aid, medical care, and supplies therefore falls on the affected country. Little effective help from international agencies is likely during the period of greatest need because of the response time required.

The management of mass casualties is divided into three main areas: search, rescue, and first aid; transport to health facilities and treatment; and redistribution of patients between hospitals when necessary.

Search, Rescue, and First Aid

After a major disaster, the need for search, rescue, and first aid is likely to be so great that organized relief services will be unable to meet more than a small fraction of the demand. Most immediate help will come from uninjured survivors, and they will have to provide whatever first aid they can. Any improvement in the quality of immediate first aid services must depend on increased instruction in them, as through Red Cross courses.

Transport to Health Facilities and Treatment

Casualties should be treated near their own homes whenever possible to avoid social dislocation and the added drain on resources of transporting them to central facilities. If there are significant medical reasons for such evacuation, the relief authority should make provision to return the patient to his or her home.

Most casualties reasonably near a health facility will generally converge on it regardless of its operating status, using whatever transport is available, but some may avoid or be unable to seek medical care, which makes active casefinding an important part of any casualty relief. This is a sufficient reason for creating mobile health-care teams in addition to fixed first aid stations located near existing health facilities.

Providing proper treatment to casualties requires that health service resources be redirected to this new priority. Bed capacity and surgical services must be expanded by selectively discharging routine inpatients, rescheduling nonpriority admissions and surgery, and using available space and personnel fully.

Normal physician responsibilities will have to be delegated extensively to nonphysicians. A center, manned 24 hours a day to respond to inquiries from patients' relatives and friends, should be established and could be staffed by able lay people. The Red Cross may be well equipped to direct this centralizing role.

If necessary, provision should be made for food and quarters for health personnel. Adequate mortuary space and services must be provided.

Triage

The mere number of casualties requiring varying degrees of medical attention in the first day after a severe disaster requires that the medical profession adopt an approach to treatment different from that they normally use.

In his *Disaster Management: Comprehensive Guidelines for Disaster Relief* (Bern, Hans Huber, 1979), Edwin H. Spirgi has clearly defined triage, or the sorting of patients in noting that "the principle of 'first come, first treated' applied in routine medical care is inadequate in mass emergencies." He continues that triage consists of rapidly classifying the injured on the basis of the benefit they can expect from medical care and not according to the severity of their injuries.

> Higher priority is granted whenever some simple intensive care may modify dramatically the immediate or long-term prognosis. Moribund patients who require much attention for a questionable benefit have the lowest priority. Triage is the only approach able to provide a maximum of benefit to most of the injured in a disaster situation.

He also notes that some physicians may consider it ethically questionable to treat patients who can be saved before the very seriously injured but dying, but that such a strategy is the only one valid for the good of the many after a disaster.

Although different triage systems have been adopted and are still in use in some countries, the most common classification consists of three categories of patients: those who cannot benefit from the treatment available under the emergency conditions; the seriously injured, who should be attended first; and patients who are ambulatory or whose injuries are less severe. After initial first aid, the last category can wait for medical attention until the seriously injured have been dealt with.

Triage should be carried out at two stages: at the disaster site in order to decide on transportation priority, and on admission to the hospital or treatment center in order to reassess the patient's needs and priority for medical attention. Ideally, local health workers should be taught the principles of triage beforehand to expedite the process when a disaster occurs. In the absence of adequate training of field health personnel, a triage officer and first aid workers must accompany all relief teams to the disaster site to make these assessments. At the hospital, triage should be the responsibility of a highly experienced clinician as it may mean life or death for the patient and will determine the activities of the whole staff.

Tagging

All patients must be identified with tags stating their name, age, sex, place of origin, triage category, diagnosis, and initial treatment. Standardized tags must be chosen or designed in advance as part of the national disaster plan. Health personnel should be thoroughly familiar with their proper use.

Organizational Structure

As Spirgi notes, effective management of mass casualties demands an organization of services quite different from that found in ordinary times. A "hospital disaster plan designates the command structure to be adopted in case of disaster," he comments. "[A] *command team* (consisting of senior officers in the medical, nursing, and administrative fields), . . . will direct people where to work according to the plan and mobilize additional staff and additional resources as required. The officer in charge . . . should have control as close to military authority as is ever seen in medical practice."

Standardized Simple Therapeutic Procedures

Treatment procedures should be economical in both human and material resources. Firstline medical treatment should be simplified and aim at saving lives and preventing major secondary complications or problems. Preparation and dissemination of standardized procedures, such as extensive debridement, delayed primary wound closure, or the use of splints instead of circular casts, can produce a marked decrease in mortality and long-term impairment. According to Spirgi,

> Such steps can be carried out quickly, in many instances by individuals with limited training. On the other hand, certain more sophisticated techniques requiring highly trained individuals and complex equipment and many supplies (e.g., as for treatment of severe burns) are not a wise investment of resources in mass casualty management. This shift in thinking and action from ordinary practice to mass medical care is not easy to achieve for many physicians.

Redistribution of Patients between Hospitals When Necessary

While health care facilities within a disaster area may be damaged and under the pressure of mass casualties, those outside may be able to cope with a much larger workload or provide specialized medical services such as neurosurgery. The decision to redistribute patients to hospitals outside the disaster area should be carefully considered since unplanned and possibly unnecessary evacuation may create more problems than it solves. Good administrative control must be maintained over any redistribution in order to restrict it to a limited number of patients in need of specialized care not available in the disaster area.

The Health Relief Coordinator should be particularly aware of the social, administrative, and legal implications of international evacuation. Medical relief teams from other countries are often unaware of existing backup facilities in the disaster-affected country and may propose transferring excess casualties or those requiring special attention to the health services of their homelands. Guidelines and policies must be clear in this regard and communicated to each relief team.

The task of matching resources to needs is best accomplished by using a chart similar to that shown in Figure 6, which can also be displayed in blowup on a wall. Hospitals are listed according to their geographic location, starting with those closest to the impact area. A visual display of the number of beds available, medical or

1 NAME-PLACE	2 Speciality	3 BEDS a Total	3 BEDS b Available	4 SURGEONS a Present	4 SURGEONS b Required	5 ANESTHESIOLOGY a Present	5 ANESTHESIOLOGY b Required	6 Other medical pers. required	7 Nurses required	8 Essential items in short supply	9 Other requirements or contracts
Hospital "A", Disaster City	general	850	8	5	4	5	4	2 pediatric, 1 gynecol.	5	suturing material, X Ray film	generator
Hospital "X", Normalville	Traumatology	450	145	5 te.	1	3	1	1 gynecol.	1	linen	limited kitchen facilities

Figure 6. Monitoring of hospital resources.

nursing personnel required for full round-the-clock services, essential medical items to direct external assistance to areas where needs and expected benefits are greatest. Patterns for redistributing resources or patients will emerge from analysis of the data. Such monitoring of hospital resources will be most useful when medical care is likely to be needed for an extended period.

If the Health Relief Coordinator finds that his country's total health care capacity is insufficient to meet disaster-related needs, several alternatives must be considered.

The best is rapid expansion of the country's own permanent facilities and staff, which has the advantage of fulfilling immediate needs and leaving behind permanent benefits.

If this is not feasible, a second alternative may be staffed, self-sufficient, mobile emergency hospitals available from governmental, military, Red Cross, or private sources. If such a hospital is necessary, one from the country itself or a neighboring country with the same language and culture should be considered first, and those from more geographically, culturally, or technologically distant countries should be considered second.

Foreign mobile hospitals may have several limitations. First, the time needed to establish a fully operational mobile hospital may be several days, though most casualties will occur as a result of the immediate impact and require treatment in the first 24 hours. Second, the cost of such a hospital, especially when airlifted, can be prohibitive and is often deducted from the total aid package given by the governmental or private relief source providing it. Third, such hospitals are often quite advanced technologically, which raises the expectations of the people they serve in a way that will be difficult if not impossible for local authorities to fulfill during the recovery period. Finally, it must be recognized that such hospitals are of great public relations value to the donor agency, which may thus press their use unsuitably.

A third alternative, the packaged disaster hospital (PDH), may be offered by several sources, but its use in the emergency phase should be considered with caution for several reasons. First, the training required to install and operate PDHs is extensive and buildings suitable for housing them must be located. It may take several weeks for such a hospital to become operational. Second, part of the material in the hospital may be obsolete, in poor condition, or unsuited to the needs of the recipient country since most such hospitals were designed in the early 1950s for use after nuclear disasters in developed nations. And third, the cost of airlifting such hospitals to a recipient country is prohibitive in relation to their benefit in relief operations.

Some of this equipment may be useful for long-term reconstruction, however. Careful study of this possibility and, ideally, on-site inspection of the equipment by the recipient agency should precede any shipment. Unless cooperating private airlines absorb its shipping cost, the equipment should be delivered by surface rather than air transportation.

Chapter 3

EPIDEMIOLOGIC SURVEILLANCE AND
DISEASE CONTROL*

Risk of Outbreak Following Disasters

Natural disasters are often followed by rumors of epidemics (typhoid fever, cholera) or unusual conditions such as increased snake bites. In fact, epidemiologists have confirmed very few such rumors when they have investigated them in the field. Whatever the rumors' lack of substance, a natural disaster may change the risk of preventable diseases. The probability of increased transmission is related to adverse changes in the following four areas:

(1) *Population density.* Closer human contact in itself increases the potential spread of airborne diseases. In addition, available sanitary services are often inadequate to cope with suddenly larger populations.

(2) *Population displacement.* The movement of disaster survivors into adjacent areas may lead to the introduction of communicable diseases to which either the migrant or indigenous populations are susceptible.

(3) *Disruption of preexisting sanitary services.* Existing sanitary facilities are often physically damaged by the natural disaster. Water supply and power systems are particularly vulnerable.

(4) *Disruption of normal public health programs.* After a disaster, personnel and funds are often diverted from essential public health programs. If such programs are not maintained or at least restored as soon as possible, communicable diseases will increase in the unprotected population.

The most frequently observed diseases in the postdisaster period are enteric ailments, which are most closely related to the first three factors above. Long-term consequences such as increased vector-borne and vaccine-preventable childhood diseases stem from the fourth factor.

The principles in preventing and controlling communicable diseases following a disaster are to (1) take all reasonable public health and administrative measures to reduce the risk of disease transmission if it is increased by one or more of the four factors; (2) investigate unconfirmed reports of disease outbreaks rapidly to prevent unnecessary dispersion of scarce resources and disruption of normal programs; and (3) organize or use a more reliable disease reporting system to identify disease outbreaks promptly, initiate control measures, and evaluate ongoing sanitary or public health programs.

---

*The assistance of Dr. Karl Western, National Institute of Allergy and Infectious Diseases, Bethesda, Maryland, USA, in preparing the final version of this chapter is most appreciated.

Setting Up a Surveillance System

Ideally, a separate postdisaster surveillance system will not be needed because a system adequate to the needs of disaster-related surveillance will already be in place. Most communities know what is happening in their own areas and have methods of sharing such information locally, but central health authorities often do not have an established mechanism for gathering this information regionally and nationally in a rational, scientific way.

It should be kept in mind that surveillance means the gathering of medical intelligence from a variety of conventional and unconventional sources. Even under normal circumstances, the institutionalized reporting system may not be the means by which important reports reach the authorities. Therefore, where a standard reporting system does not exist or exists only rudimentarily, it is fruitless to try to establish or improve one in the immediate postdisaster period. The Health Relief Coordinator should recognize that newspaper accounts and information from political sources, for example, may be as or more important than standard health data channels. Unconventional information must be used and should include community sources.

Postdisaster information collection systems fall into three categories—existing standard surveillance, unofficial community sources, and relief worker reports. From an administrative viewpoint, data from all these systems must be routed directly to the Health Relief Coordinator so that appropriate actions can be taken in the most expeditious manner. For the most part, data will be qualitative rather than quantitative.

In order to collect, collate, and interpret the data, a national epidemiologist with adequate epidemiologic and clerical staff who have transportation to the field and priority access to public or private laboratory facilities will be essential. In addition to the national epidemiologic staff, university departments, research centers, and bilateral or international agencies may provide trained epidemiologists and laboratory support nationally or regionally. A national epidemiologist should be the secretary of a disease surveillance and control subcommittee of the health relief committee including senior representatives of the health ministry, sanitation and water services, major accredited voluntary agencies, and other ministries involved in health relief programs. Summary reports of the surveillance system's technical findings can be made through this subcommittee and appropriate action taken to introduce the necessary control measures if beyond the immediate competence of the epidemiologists (large sanitation programs, for example), and to disseminate to the general public and abroad reports on the risks, occurrence, and nonoccurrence of disease by radio and other media through the national emergency committee. The subcommittee can provide direct feedback to hospitals and other health facilities where surveillance data are being collected.

Disease Surveillance

Under normal conditions, surveillance systems include diseases which are endemic to the area, amenable to control, of public ehalth importance, or are internationally notifiable. If such an effort has normally existed, it should continue through the disaster whenever possible. Where surveillance did not exist or has broken down as a direct consequence of disaster, a more focused, symptom-based surveillance system should be instituted. It should concentrate on diseases that are likely to be produced by the disaster or are particularly amenable to control.

The national epidemiologist and the Health Relief Coordinator should designate symptom complexes or diseases to be included in this system. Symptom complexes which might be important include fever, fever and diarrhea, fever and cough, trauma, burns, and measles. All patient facilities should institute this system. Reporting units actually increase their reporting when it is simplified and targeted as described, using a standardized form (see example in Figure 7). It is the respon-

Figure 7.

DISEASE SURVEILLANCE DAILY REPORT

Symptoms or clearly recognizable diseases

Health facility
or
relief team .... Date: ....

	CASES		DEATHS	
	Under 15 yrs.	Over 15 yrs.	Under 15 yrs.	Over 15 yrs.
Fever (no diarrhea/cough)[1]				
Fever with diarrhea[2]				
Fever with cough[3]				
Measles				
Meningitis				
Dog bite				
Snake bite				
Burns				
Trauma				
Protein-energy malnutrition				
Other				
Daily total				

Comments: _____

[1]Indicative of malaria, dengue
[2]Can be subdivided on basis of blood, mucus, vomiting
[3]Indicative of respiratory infections

26

sibility of the national epidemiologist to distribute, explain, and supervise the collection ot these forms. This, in addition to prompt feedback to reporting units, should overcome their reluctance to participate.

Presentation and Interpretation of Collected Data

From the above, it is obvious that postdisaster surveillance will not provide precise information on the incidence of a disease. Rates (the number of cases in a known population) are difficult enough to determine under normal conditions and probably impossible and not worth the effort after disaster. What will be possible is an indication that a given symptom complex or disease is occurring in an affected area. This indication will provide the basis for a more intensive investigation, and if necessary lead to specific control measures. Where the affected population is well defined, as in refugee camps, rates will be important for the national epidemiologist to determine.

If the above system is effective, it will invariably result in an increase in the number of reported common and uncommon diseases because the number of reporting units and public awareness and concern are increased. This is not necessarily a reflection of increased disease, but rather a result of increased disease discovery over the predisaster ascertainment pattern.

Because negative reports are as important as positive ones, each reporting unit should submit reports whether or not it has seen any disease. Negative reports will show that the unit is functioning and that health-care resources can be channeled elsewhere.

The epidemiologist closest to the local reporting unit should investigate suspected disease outbreaks detected by the surveillance system as soon as possible. Until epidemiologic assistance arrives, initial investigation and control measures are the responsibility of the local health unit. Before a disaster, the national epidemiologist should formulate guidelines and disseminate them to reporting units and field health facilities for use in investigating an controlling basic symptom complexes once disaster strikes.

Laboratory Services

Access to accurate, discrete, and rapid laboratory services is essential for public health management, but the number of laboratory tests required will not be great. If such access to local laboratories cannot be guaranteed, alternate and perhaps reference laboratory assistance may be required. Some diagnostic tests (ova and parasites in stools, blood smears) can be made with a minimum of appropriate technology by field reporting units, but certain bacteriologic and virologic tests necessary for surveillance must be performed by referral laboratories.

Vaccination and Vaccination Programs

Medical authorities are often under considerable public and political pressure to begin mass vaccination programs, usually against typhoid, cholera, and tetanus. This pressure may be increased by exaggerated reporting of the risks of such diseases in the local and international press, and by the ready availability of vaccines from abroad.

Typhoid and Cholera

Rapidly improvised mass vaccination campaigns against typhoid and cholera should be avoided for several reasons:

(1) No documented large-scale outbreaks have occurred following natural disasters.

(2) The World Health Organization does not recommend typhoid and cholera vaccines for routine use in endemic areas. Typhoid and cholera vaccines offer only low and short-term individual protection and little protection against the spread of disease. Higher and longer-lived protection will occur naturally in endemic areas where the population has previously been exposed to disease, but it will still be insufficient to prevent the spread of disease. Good medical control must rest on effective case identification, isolation, and treatment.

(3) Complete coverage of the population is probably impossible to achieve in a reasonable time, even if only a single dose is to be given. It will be more difficult to obtain adequate coverage with a second or third dose later when public concern has diminished. Experience has generally been that adequate registration of vaccinated individuals is impossible under emergency conditions, which makes systematic followup impossible. This problem is compounded if several agencies conduct vaccination programs without communication or coordination, in some cases disregarding government policies in the matter.

(4) Vaccination programs require large numbers of workers who could be better employed elsewhere.

(5) The quality of vaccine available, particularly if obtained rapidly from unusual sources, is often unsatisfactory.

(6) Unless vaccination can be done without needles, as by using high-pressure injectors, mass vaccination is likely to mean the reuse of inadequately sterilized needles which may transmit hepatitis B. Even if disposable equipment is available, adequate supervision of the injection technique may be impossible.

(7) Mass vaccination programs may lead to a false sense of security about the risk of disease and to the neglect of effective control measures.

The paratyphoid AB component of mixed vaccines (TAB vaccine) is ineffective and gives little if any individual protection.

Tetanus

Two preparations are available for protection against tetanus. The first is tetanus toxoid, which is an effective immunizing agent used routinely in children and women of childbearing age. The best protection against tetanus is maintenance of a high level of immunity in the general population by routine vaccination before disaster and adequate and early wound cleansing. If a high level of immunity has been maintained in a patient who has sustained an open wound, tetanus toxoid booster is an effective preventive measure. The second preparation, tetanus antitoxin, should be administered only at the discretion of a physician to previously unimmunized wounded patients.

Significant increases in tetanus have not occurred after natural disasters. The mass vaccination of populations against tetanus using tetanus toxoid is unnecessary and cannot be expected to reduce the risk of tetanus in casualties.

Vaccination programs may be justified in camps and other densely populated areas with large numbers of young children whose vaccination against measles, whooping cough, and possibly poliomyelitis and diphtheria might be advisable, and where routine vaccination programs, as against diphtheria and measles, are normally conducted. If administrative arrangements remain adequate, the opportunity may be taken to continue routine programs by vaccinating appropriate age groups. This may allay public fears.

Vaccine Importation and Storage

Most vaccines—and particularly measles vaccine—require refrigeration and careful handling if they are to remain effective. If cold-chain facilities are inadequate, they should be requested at the same time as vaccines. Vaccine donors should ensure that adequate refrigeration facilities exist in the country before dispatching vaccines. During the emergency period it may be advisable for all imported vaccines, including those for voluntary agencies, to be consigned to government stocks.

The vaccination policy to be adopted should be decided at the national level only. Individual voluntary agencies should not decide to vaccinate on their own. Ideally, a national policy should be articulated as part of the predisaster plan.

Chapter 4

ENVIRONMENTAL HEALTH MANAGEMENT*

Priorities

Environmental health is of primary importance in emergency health management after a natural disaster. Technical details can be found in M. Assar, *A Guide to Sanitation in Natural Disasters* (Geneva, World Health Organization, 1971).

Within the affected area, these activities should be directed at specific locales in the following order:

Population density	Extent of disruption of preexisting services	Priority
Dense	Severe	I
Dense	Moderate	II
Sparse	Severe	
Sparse	Minor	III

In deciding what action will have to be taken, the following factors should be considered:

Priority Areas for Intervention

First consideration should be given to those areas in which health risks have increased. Priority should be given to urban peripheries, camps, and temporary settlements.

Priority Environmental Health Services

Primary consideration should be given to services essential for protecting and ensuring the well-being of people in high-risks areas. Postdisaster environmental health measures can be divided into two priorities. The first is adequate quantities of safe water, basic sanitation facilities, disposal of excreta and liquid and solid wastes, and shelter. The second priority consists of food protection measures, establishing or continuing vector-control measures, and promoting personal hygiene.

Manpower

The availability of appropriate environmental health specialists will be a limiting factor when trying to manage an emergency situation. First consideration should

*The contribution of Mr. Pierre Leger, Director, International Division, Medical Care Development, in preparing the final version of this chapter is most appreciated.

therefore be given to using locally available manpower. The local population should be actively involved and its cooperation sought in providing needed services. It should be clear that all immediate or short-term activities are directed to restoring predisaster environmental services. Improvement in environmental services should not be the aim of immediate disaster relief. Experts such as foreign relief workers who are unfamiliar with preexisting local environmental services may provide poor advice on relief priorities.

A checklist of possible disruptions in environmental health services is presented in Table 2.

Table 2. Natural disasters effects matrix.

	Most common effects on environmental health	Earthquake	Hurricane/ Tornado	Flood	Tsunamis
Water supply and waste-water disposal	Damage to civil engineering structures	●	●	●	○
	Broken mains	●	◐	◐	○
	Power outages	●	●	◐	◐
	Contamination (biological or chemical)	◐	●	●	●
	Transportation failures	●	●	●	◐
	Personnel shortages	●	◐	◐	○
	System overloading (due to shifts in population)	○	●	●	○
	Equipment, parts, and supply shortages	●	●	●	◐
Solid waste handling	Damage to civil engineering structures	●	◐	◐	○
	Transportation failures	●	●	●	◐
	Equipment shortages	●	●	●	◐
	Personnel shortages	●	●	●	○
	Water, soil, and air pollution	●	●	●	◐
Food handling	Damage to food preparation facilities	●	●	◐	○
	Transportation failures	●	●	●	◐
	Power outages	●	●	◐	◐
	Flooding of facilities	○	●	●	●
	Contamination/degradation of relief supplies	◐	●	●	◐
Vector control	Proliferation of vector breeding sites	●	●	●	●
	Increase in human-vector contacts	●	●	●	◐
	Disruption of vector-borne disease control programs	●	●	●	●
Home sanitation	Destruction or damage to structures	●	●	●	●
	Contamination of water and food	◐	◐	●	◐
	Disruption of power, heating, fuel, water, or supply waste disposal services	●	●	●	◐
	Overcrowding	○	○	○	○

● Severe possible effect.
◐ Less severe possible effect.
○ Least or no possible effect.

31

To guarantee safe and sufficient water supplies, adequate shelter, and basic sanitation facilities in the stricken area, particularly for refugees, the following environmental health measures are recommended:

(1) Make an initial survey to determine the extent of damage to public water supply, waste disposal, and food production, storage, and distribution systems.

(2) Make an inventory of available resources such as undamaged food stocks, manpower, and readily available materials, equipment, and supplies.

(3) Obtain information on population movements in or near the area such as refugee camps, partially or totally evacuated areas, and relief worker settlements. This information should determine the areas to be given priority based on population density and high risk of disease.

(4) Determine the stricken population's immediate needs of water, basic sanitation facilities, and housing.

(5) Meet the needs of essential users as quickly as possible after basic human consumption needs are satisfied. Hospitals and other medical facilities, for example, may need much more water because of the large number of casualties to be treated, as will any remaining power plants for their operation.

(6) Ensure that refugees are properly housed and refugee centers have basic necessities such as safe water and food supplies, excreta disposal units, and facilities for solid waste disposal.

(7) Ensure that certain high-risk areas, such as those with dense population, are supplied with safe water supplies and emergency excreta facilities.

These measures will entail actions in the following areas:

Water Supply

A survey of all public water supplies will have to be made, giving priority to drinking water distribution systems. It will have to be determined if the water supply has been contaminated by things such as sewage plant effluents. If a potential chemical contaminant such as heavy metals from volcanic eruptions is suspected, alternate water sources should be sought. The water should be analyzed as soon as possible. If bacterial contaminants are found, the water supply should be disinfected before distribution by increasing residual chlorine and pressure in the distribution system.

When repairs are undertaken, first priority should be given to repairing and restoring water supply systems. It is recommended that all repaired mains, reservoirs, treatment tanks, or other units should be properly cleaned and disinfected.

Systematic chlorination of all wells and rain water systems is not essential unless they have to be repaired or cleaned. Many of these structures may have been unsanitary before the disaster, and their disinfection will be of limited value and not an effective use of resources unless the population concentration they serve has changed. For example, if a refugee camp is next to a well, consideration should be given to converting it to a properly protected well as quickly as possible.

If the water distribution system is partially damaged, emergency water supplies can be drawn from one point of the distribution system and hauled to waterless areas. Water tankers may be obtained locally from commercial water delivery, bulk milk, and water, brewery, and milk bottling plant truck fleets. As a general rule, the adaptation of gasoline, chemical, or sewage trucks should be avoided as a means of transporting water. All trucks should be inspected to determine their fitness, and they should be cleaned and disinfected before being used as emergency water carriers.

Private water supply systems or sources often exist in the vicinity of a disaster-stricken community. These systems may belong to dairies, breweries, food and beverage plants, and other industrial or agricultural establishments. The source of supply is often a deep well or private treatment plant. With adequate chlorination, water from such sources can be hauled to emergency distribution points.

If locally available, mobile water purification plants may be used in emergencies. Such units can produce only limited amounts of drinking water and require skilled workers for operation, however. They should not be given priority consideration, particularly when the large amount of space and money required to transport and operate them might be better used to procure more essential emergency supplies.

The *mass distribution* of tablet, powder, or liquid disinfectants should only be considered when it can be coupled with a vigorous health education campaign to instruct people how to use them; distribution of water storage containers; the assistance of public health or auxiliary workers to ensure proper and continued use of the tablets, and a distribution network to ensure additional supplies as needed throughout the emergency phase and into the early rehabilitation phase.

In general, *individuals* in limited and controlled groups may be given such disinfectants to purify small amounts of drinking water for one or two weeks. Every effort should be made to restore normal chlorination facilities or to protect individual wells and cisterns through physical measures such as sealing cracks in well casings or improving drainage around a well.

Basic Sanitation

Unless they have had no prior experience with them, emergency latrines should be made available to residents, refugees, and relief workers in areas where such facilities have been destroyed. Solid waste collection or sanitary disposal systems should be developed for stricken areas. Burying or burning solid waste is recommended. The general public should be informed about sanitary waste handling where no service is available.

Vector Control

Rain or flood waters on the soil, in empty receptacles, and elsewhere, in addition to the unsanitary conditions they create by trapping debris and solid wastes, cause insects and rodents to proliferate. Controlling vector-borne diseases should be the aim of activities taken during an emergency, especially in areas where such diseases are known to be prevalent. Vector-control measures should be associated with other health measures such as malaria chemoprophylaxis to reduce or eliminate the risks of infection.

Essential vector-control measures in emergencies are as follows:

(1) Inform the public of measures they should take to eliminate breeding sites and otherwise protect themselves against vector-borne diseases.

(2) Survey camps and other densely populated areas to identify potential mosquito breeding sites.

(3) Eliminate breeding sites permanently as much as possible by draining, filling, overturning receptacles, etc.

(4) Resume indoor spraying, if used earlier as a routine control method, in flooded areas.

(5) Well-organized mosquito breeding site control greatly reduces the need for outdoor spraying, but if surveys show its need, local resources should be employed. The use of sophisticated equipment and supplies is not recommended because of their high cost and short, scant benefit.

(6) Dust refugees in camps and temporary settlements in areas where typhus is known to exist.

Successfully controlling houseflies and rodents is nearly impossible in the early aftermath of a natural disaster. The only acceptable measures against them are environmental sanitation and personal hygiene. Water and food should be stored in closed areas. Refuse and other solid waste should be cleaned up and disposed of sanitarily as soon as possible, for that is the most effective way to control the spread of such pests.

Personal Hygiene

Personal hygiene tends to decline after natural disasters, especially in densely populated areas such as refugee settlements. The following environmental health measures are recommended: provide refugees with washing, cleaning, and bathing facilities; make water available to people living away from settlements whose supply has been interrupted; avoid overcrowding in sleeping quarters, and inform people about and encourage them to attend to personal hygiene.

Burial of the Dead

Public health authorities may find themselves directly responsible for or asked advice about the health hazards attendant on the disposal of bodies. The health hazards associated with unburied bodies are minimal. Especially if death resulted from trauma, bodies are quite unlikely to cause outbreaks of diseases such as typhoid fever, cholera, or plague, though they may transmit gastroenteritis or food poisoning syndrome to survivors if they contaminate streams, wells, or other water sources.

Despite the negligible health risk, dead bodies represent a delicate social problem. The normal local method of burial or cremation should be used whenever possible. Burial is the simplest and best method if it is ritually acceptable and physically possible. Cremation is not justified on health grounds, and mass cremations require large amounts of fuel.

Before disposal, bodies must be identified and the identifications recorded.

In many countries, certification of death or an autopsy must precede the disposal of bodies. Incorporating a waiver paragraph in legislation governing disaster emergencies should be considered.

General Public Information

Besides the specifics already mentioned in previous sections, information about available environmental health services and resources and their location, refugee camps, and what authorities ought to be notified of problems should also be given to the public. This helps the public understand the extent of the emergency, reduces confusion, and improves the effectiveness of emergency environmental health activities.

Chapter 5

FOOD AND NUTRITION*

Not all acute disasters produce food shortages severe enough to cause harmful changes in the nutritional status of the population. The nature of the problems that arise will depend on the type, duration, and extent of the disaster, as well as the food and nutritional conditions existing in the area before the catastrophe. Large-scale food distribution is not always an immediate relief priority, and its long-term implementation may in fact produce undesired effects.

To determine what kind of food relief is needed and when, Health Relief Coordinators should be familiar with the expected outcomes of specific types of disasters. This rule of thumb must then be modified according to the circumstances in their particular area. The primary steps involved in assuring that a food relief program will be effective are assessing the food supplies available after disaster, gauging the nutritional needs of the affected population, calculating the daily food rations and needs for large population groups, and, finally, monitoring the nutritional status of the affected population. The nutrition officer, who is trained in these areas, must be consulted and included in relief planning and implementation.

Expected Consequences of Disasters

The most likely consequence of any kind of disaster will be the disruption of transportation and communications systems and upheavals in routine social and economic activities. As a result, even when food stocks exist, they may often be inaccessible due to the disorganization of the distribution system or the loss of income with which to buy food. When destruction of a greater magnitude occurs, leading to the death of livestock and the loss of crops and stocks, the short-term dilemma can leave a more severe, long-term crisis in its wake. Moreover, evacuation and resettlement of communities during the postdisaster period are often necessary, creating foci in which total food supplies will have to be provided for the duration of the encampment. Hospitals and other institutions may require emergency food supplies as well.

Although the situations described above can occur after any disaster, some differences in the long- and short-term effects may be expected depending on the type. Earthquake, for example, generally have little direct impact on the long-term total availability of food. Standing crops are unaffected, and food stocks can sometimes be salvaged from family, wholesale, and retail stores. Temporary food problems, on the other hand, may result as an indirect consequence of the breakdown of the transportation and marketing systems. If an earthquake strikes during a labor-intensive period such as a harvest, the loss of labor from death and its diversion from agriculture may cause similar short-term scarcities.

---

*The contributions of Drs. Miguel Gueri and Curtis McIntosh, of the Caribbean Food and Nutrition Institute, in preparing this chapter are most appreciated.

In contrast to earthquakes, hurricanes, floods, and sea surges affect food availability directly. Standing crops may be completely destroyed and, especially if there is no warning period, seed stores and family food stocks may also be lost.

Possible Adverse Effects of Large-scale Food Distribution

The decision to distribute large amounts of food should be made at the highest level and be based on the most accurate information available. If unnecessarily large quantities of food are brought into an area, this may hinder recovery. Food distribution requires transport and personnel that may be better employed in other ways and small farmers may face hardship due to depressed market prices. Perhaps the most serious side effect is that maintaining a population by free food distribution, if not accompanied by the essentials such as seeds and tools needed to restart the local economy, may create dependence on relief.

Setting Priorities

The priorities in alleviating food problems are to: (1) supply food immediately where there appears to be an urgent need, namely to isolated populations, institutions, and relief workers; (2) make an initial estimate of likely food needs in the area so that steps can be taken toward procurement, transport, storage, and distribution; (3) locate or procure stocks of food and assess their fitness for consumption; and (4) monitor information on food needs so that procurement, distribution, and other programs can be modified as the situation changes.

Immediate Relief

During the first few, usually chaotic days after a disaster strikes, the exact extent of the damage is unknown, communications are difficult, and the number of people affected seems to double by the hour. Food distribution must start as soon as possible, but because of the large variety and small stocks of commodities sent in by governments, agencies, private organizations, and individuals, food distribution is initially a day-to-day exercise. Planning logical food rations during this period is impossible. What matters during this "chaotic stage" is to get a minimum of 6.7 to 8.4 Megajoules (1,600 to 2,000 kcal) a day to everybody, in whatever form, whether it be apple sauce, liver paste, or carrots. For very short-term need—one week or so—an emergency ration of about 7 Megajoules (1,700 kcal) will prevent severe nutritional deterioration and mass starvation.

As an immediate relief step, available food should be distributed to any group that is at high risk, or appears to be wanting, in sufficient quantity (3 or 4 kg per person) to ensure survival for one week. Food should be included automatically, for example, in supplies sent to communities isolated by earthquake or displaced by flooding. Where fuel shortages are likely, it may be better to distribute cooked food such as boiled rice or bread rather than dry food.

No detailed calculation need be made of the precise vitamin, mineral, or protein content in the first two or three weeks, but supplies should be acceptable and palatable. The most important thing that must be provided is sufficient energy. If no other items can be obtained, distribution of a cereal alone will be sufficient to meet basic nutritional requirements. When a population can find some of its own food, it may be possible to confine distribution to a single item such as beans and supply only part of the ration.

Estimating Food Requirements

As soon as possible after a disaster, a first rough estimate should be made of likely bulk food items needed. This will enable managers to take the necessary steps to locate and procure stocks, storage, and transport.

In the absence of detailed information, the food requirements estimate must be based to some extent on judgment, but it should take into account the following factors: (1) the probable effect of the disaster on food availability (e.g., a sea surge may have destroyed all household supplies); (2) the approximate size of the population affected; (3) normal food supply and variations within the area (e.g., the approximate percentages of the population who are subsistence farmers and those who depend wholly on purchased food); and (4) the impact of seasonal factors. In subsistence areas just before the harvest, for instance, household and traders' stocks may be depleted and the population may be more dependent on the market.

The nutrition officer should prepare estimates of foods on the basis of a family (usually considered five people) for one week and one month. Food distribution on a family basis for periods of one month may be considered, logistically, the most practical system. The nutrition officer should also prepare estimates of commodities required by large population groups; for instance, on the basis of 1,000 people for one month. Two simple and useful rules of thumb are: (1) 16 metric tons of food sustain 1,000 people for one month, and (2) to store one metric ton of food, about two cubic meters of space is needed. Proper storage is extremely important to avoid food losses due to rain, pests, or looting.

When calculating the composition of daily rations, the following points should be kept in mind: (1) the ration should be kept as simple as possible; (2) to facilitate storage and distribution, nonperishable food commodities that are not bulky should be chosen; and (3) substitution of items within food groups should be allowed for.

The food ration should be based on three groups of foods, a staple, preferably a cereal; a concentrated energy source such as a fat; and concentrated source of protein.

Whenever possible, vulnerable groups should receive a food supplement in addition to the basic diet. In this group we include children under five years, who are growing very fast and may suffer permanent damage if malnourished, and pregnant and lactating women, who require more nutrients. Breastmilk is the best food for infants under six months, and Health Relief Coordinators should not allow the emergency situation to become an excuse for flooding the country with infant formulas.

Procurement

If the calculated amount of food required exceeds immediate local availability and it is anticipated that food will have to be distributed for several months, steps must be taken to obtain food from elsewhere in the country or abroad. A rough estimate of local food transport requirements should also be made for this contingency.

Food for the initial emergency distribution phase should be obtained from national government or wholesaler stocks, or from bilateral or international development agencies.

If large quantities of food are required from abroad, procurement and shipping may require several months. Approaches to suitable agencies should hence be made at the earliest possible date. It is critical that Health Relief Coordinators advise potential donors of the eating habits and preferences of their populations. Food not eaten will provide no nutritional benefit.

The need for special infant foods ("baby foods") immediately after disasters is often exaggerated. Improving maternal nutrition and assisting mothers economically is more cost-effective and safer than airlifting strained baby foods. Since vitamin requirements are of no concern during the acute emergency phase, multivitamin tablets should not be requested as a separate relief item.

Surveillance

If long-term food supply problems seem likely, as in areas with subsistence agriculture and poor communications, the nutritional status of the community should be monitored. This can be accomplished by making regular physical measurements of a suitable sample of the population. Since young children are the most sensitive to nutritional changes, the surveillance system should be based on them, remembering that the most serious malnutrition results from an acute exacerbation of chronic undernutrition. In emergency situations, weight for height will provide the best indicator of acute changes in nutritional status, although arm circumference, which is simple and easy, can also be used.

As the results of the first surveys of need become available, more accurate information will make it possible to adjust preliminary estimates of the proportion of the population most in need of long-term distribution. Surveys of need should make sure to cover not only food availability, but also identify areas where problems of labor, tools, marketing, and other variables affecting distribution have arisen. As soon as an area is able to return to normal consumption patterns, distribution should be phased out.

Technical details of food distribution and feeding techniques can be found in C. de Ville de Goyet, J. Seaman, and U. Geiger, *The Management of Nutritional Emergencies in Large Populations* (Geneva, World Health Organization, 1978), and Protein-Calorie Advisory Group of the United Nations System, *A Guide to Food and Health Relief Operations for Disasters* (New York, United Nations, 1977).

Chapter 6

MANAGEMENT OF HEALTH RELIEF SUPPLIES

During the first week, health relief supplies will consist mainly of drugs and medical equipment for treating casualties and preventing communicable disease. Later supplies will include sanitary engineering equipment, vehicles, food, construction materials, and the like.

Immediate needs must be met primarily by the affected country, its closest neighbors, or well-equipped foreign armed forces. Emergency supplies that must come from abroad are often limited to few essential items of relatively small bulk.

Although some consignments of medical supplies will arrive at the main airport within 24 hours, their unloading, sorting, and delivery to the site of need is likely to take much longer. The bulk of relief supplies is usually received after most urgent health needs have been met with limited local means.

In summary, the main problem is not acquiring large amounts of new supplies but redistributing those on hand.

Use of Local Stocks

Every country has normal operating stocks of drugs and other medical supplies in hospital stores, government and commercial warehouses, and military stockpiles. These supplies in and outside the affected area are often large enough to meet immediate drug needs in the emergency period, for even if warehouses have been damaged some stock may still be salvageable.

Localized shortages arise in the emergency period because of the difficulty of locating and transporting material within the disaster area and the disproportionately high consumption of items such as x-ray film, casting plaster, and dressings.

The effective mobilization of all local sources of medicine and medical supplies will require that the Health Relief Coordinator update or establish a rough inventory of the types of supplies available and their location and condition following the impact, have the authority to purchase or requisition them from private suppliers, and reallocate budgeted funds to meet immediate needs.

National List of Essential Drugs

A World Health Organization expert committee has stated:

For the optimal use of limited financial resources the available drugs must be restricted to those called essential drugs indicating that they are of utmost importance, and are basic, indispensable and necessary for the health needs of the population. (*The Selection of Essential Drugs; First Report of the WHO Expert Committee.* Geneva, World Health Organization, 1977. WHO Technical Report Series No. 615. Page 9.)

This approach, recommended for normal conditions, is becoming critical for health management in emergency situations.

UNICEF, the League of Red Cross Societies, the World Health Organization and its affiliated Pan American Health Organization, and some governmental relief agencies have developed lists of essential drugs for disaster relief. Although each list is designed to meet the specific needs and relief functions of the organization or countries served, they have common characteristics. The drugs included in the lists for disaster situations are chosen from the World Health Organization's model list of essential drugs for normal conditions (about 200 generic names), proven to be therapeutically effective, useful in dealing with a clinical or public health problem of particular significance following a disaster, and limited in diversity and numbers (generally under 50 preparations).

Internationally compiled lists should only serve as a model. Every disaster-prone country should prepare in advance its own list of basic medical supplies to be made available immediately through local stockpiling, increases in inventory in pharmaceutical stores or government hospitals, or donation following a major catastrophe.

Submitting Requests for International Assistance

Since some essential items may be in short supply at the time of impact and drug stocks and budgets will rapidly be depleted and insufficient to initiate early rehabilitation and reestablish normal primary health care, assistance will be required from abroad.

To maximize the benefit of scarce international assistance to the country, the following guidelines should be followed:

(1) A single government official should be made responsible for channeling emergency international requests, for otherwise duplication, confusion, and shortcomings will result.

(2) Potential donors should be asked to provide large amounts of a few items since this simplifies and expedites procurement and shipping.

(3) The request should clearly indicate the order of priority, amounts, and formulation (e.g., tablets or syrup). Vague requests for "antidiarrheal drugs," "antibiotics," or "vaccines" must be avoided. The amounts requested should be compatible with the size of the affected population and the anticipated occurrence of trauma and disease. Requests that foreign agencies and governments have considered out of proportion to the magnitude of the disaster have proved counterproductive.

(4) Requests should be limited to drugs of proven therapeutic value and reasonable cost. Emergency situations are hardly a justification for requesting expensive and sophisticated drugs (especially antibiotics) and equipment which the country could not afford before the disaster.

(5) Perishable products and vaccines should not be requested unless refrigeration facilities are available and special handling arrangements can be made at the airport.

(6) Supplies will be duplicated if the same list is sent to several donors. Some items may be shipped by a number of suppliers and others not at all. The World Health Organization can help the country to assess its needs more precisely and inform donors of the most appropriate assistance. Occasional failure to coordinate relief supply donations nationally has resulted in time-consuming direct consulta-

tions between governments willing to assist, relief agencies, UNDRO, and the World Health Organization to determine their respective courses of action.

Some donor countries and agencies are reluctant to replace local medical stocks which have been used for emergency purposes and instead want to supply emergency needs directly. This problem is reduced if suppliers are informed that local stocks depleted during the emergency will not allow the rehabilitation of normal medical services. Donors should also realize that their consignments of supplies often cannot be received and distributed in time to be used in treating casualties.

Procedures for Labeling and Marking Consignments*

Long experience in different international relief operations has shown that all agencies need to use a uniform system for marking or labeling relief consignments. Recipient governments and donors should adopt the procedures the League of Red Cross Societies has developed in coordination with United Nations agencies.

(1) *Color code.* The colors used for the relief supplies most often required after disasters are: red for foodstuffs, blue for clothing and household equipment, and green for medical supplies and equipment.

(2) *Labeling.* Consignments of medicines, banded with green, should tell on the outside of the package the medicines' expiration date and whatever temperature controls are necessary. English should be used on all labels and stenciled markings, though a second language may be added. It is essential that the final destination (or arrival port) appear at the bottom of the label in very large letters.

(3) *Size and weight.* Containers should be of a size and weight that one man can handle (ideally, 25 kg; up to a maximum of 50 kg) since mechanical loading and unloading devices are rarely available at the receiving end.

(4) *Contents.* Relief supplies should always be packed by type in separate containers. Mixed consignments create many problems in warehousing and ultimate distribution at the receiving end. The color code recommended loses its value if medical supplies are packed in the same container as food, for instance.

(5) *Advance notice to the consignee and Health Relief Coordinator.* To cover in one document all the details necessary for safe transport and ease of handling at the receiving end, the following information is essential: (1) name of sender; (2) name of consignee; (3) method of transport, including (where applicable) the name of the vessel or flight number and its date and port or airport of departure; (4) a detailed list of contents, including weight, dimensions, and number and type of packages; (5) value in the currency of the sending country; (6) type of insurance, name of company, etc.; (7) the carrier's agent, including the name of the person to be contacted in the receiving country; (8) estimated time of arrival (ETA); and (9) instructions or special requirements for handling and storing the supplies. It should be noted that in most instances a *pro forma* invoice is required by the authorities in the sending or receiving country or both.

(6) *Acknowledgment by the receiving country.* It is important that an acknowledgment be sent to donors as quickly as possible after consignments are received.

---

*Abstracted from Annex 8, *Red Cross Disaster Relief Handbook* (Geneva, League of Red Cross Societies, 1976).

Inventory and Distribution of Incoming Supplies

Though most major international suppliers respond only to specific requests from the national government concerned, some smaller agencies and private individuals dispatch medical supplies on their own initiative.

Unsolicited drug supplies are often a major problem in large relief operations. Quantities may be very large (over 100 tons in one recorded instance) and vary greatly in quality: small quantities of mixed drugs, free samples, used or expired medicines, and drugs identified only by brand names or in a foreign language.

Critical supplies sent at the request of the affected country will compete for storage space and transport with the bulk (up to 90 per cent) of unsolicited supplies of little value. The receiving government should adopt a firm policy about accepting unsolicited, unannounced supplies. This policy statement should in general suggest that international assistance not be sent except in response to a specific request from or after negotiation with the national government. National representatives abroad and local diplomatic missions and aid agencies should be informed of the policy.

When possible, professional inspection of medical supplies collected from the private sector abroad should be arranged before shipment.

Despite any such policy, the arrival of unsolicited supplies should be anticipated and procedures devised to handle them. A health ministry representative should be at the airport to examine consignments, separate out identifiable ones suitable for immediate use, and designate storage points for all others. Consignments should be sorted immediately only if that does not hamper operations or divert professional manpower from more productive tasks. Pharmacy students have proved useful and have gained valuable experience in sorting out medicines.

Some arriving medical supplies will be addressed directly to national and international nongovernmental agencies working in the country. In the immediate postdisaster period it is probably more practical to release them directly to the agency concerned than to attempt the considerable task of centralizing drug storage and distribution. Vaccines ought to be excepted since vaccination programs should at all stages remain under government direction and control (see Chapter 3).

Distribution will be facilitated if incoming drugs are classified and labeled according to therapeutic classes and priority need (e.g., life saving, important, miscellaneous).

Expired Drugs, Perishable Products

Some drugs close to or past their stated expiration dates are often donated or offered. Expiration dates are very conservatively set for some drugs, and with suitable storage the drugs remain safe and potent for much longer. When consignments are large and the drug is of particular value, reference laboratory testing and recertification should be arranged. Assistance may be requested from the United Nations or bilateral sources.

Whole blood is often donated from abroad, although its medical need is generally limited. International donors of blood should check that a need exists, it cannot be met locally, and adequate refrigeration facilities are available. Unrefrigerated blood consignments should be destroyed. It is more convenient to request or donate equipment to collect blood or a suitable supply of blood substitutes.

Large amounts of intravenous fluids such as glucosaline are generally flown into the disaster area on the country's request. The need for IV solutions is often overstated in disaster situations and, in most cases, alternate methods of treatment are as effective, safer, and more economical. An example is oral rehydration solutions for diarrhea cases.

Delays in delivery and the high cost of air freight are additional factors to weigh before submitting a request or placing an urgent package order. Expenditures for air freight incurred by donors are generally subtracted from the overall amount they allocate for a given disaster. Funds spent on airlift are not available for other relief purposes.

Chapter 7

PLANNING, LAYOUT, AND MANAGEMENT OF TEMPORARY SETTLEMENTS AND REFUGEE CAMPS

Health authorities will not usually be directly responsible for setting up and managing camps and temporary settlements. Since many aspects of camp management affect the health of the occupants, however, the Health Relief Coordinator should be involved in decision making as early as possible.

Planning of Settlements and Camps

Temporary settlements or more permanent camps arise in a number of ways.

After floods, people can be forced to move to higher dry ground. Such settlements often disband spontaneously when flood waters retreat, but may become long-standing if a flood seriously damages agricultural or building land.

After earthquakes or destructive winds, some of the people who have lost their own houses may be unable to find lodging with relatives and friends. When aftershocks occur and a continuing risk is perceived, people often move into open spaces, parks, and fields. Land formerly inhabited by the poor may be unusable for housing after earthquakes. People in rented homes may find their landlords reluctant or slow to rebuild or that replacement rental housing is too expensive.

Assistance should be provided to people in or at the site of their homes. Whenever possible, the deliberate creation of camps should be avoided. More problems will generally be created than are solved because camps and temporary settlements present the greatest potential for communicable diseases once the immediate disaster has passed and often become permanent even when that is not intended.

In a sense, these two points conflict since it might be expected that providing services to a camp would encourage the population to stay and become dependent on relief. Though this may become true after long periods, it is unusual in the short term. People generally prefer to return to their normal lives and surroundings, and when they become dependent on relief it is usually for want of an alternative.

Setting Up Camps and Settlements

There are two objects in setting up camps and settlements. The first is to ensure a standard of living for the inhabitants as close as possible to that among similar groups in the country outside camps. Particularly in temporary settlements, voluntary workers and agencies often tend to provide much better services, food, and housing than the occupants knew before and will have after the emergency. This causes friction with the surrounding population and gives the refugees expectations which the national authorities cannot possibly meet. The second is to minimize both capital and recurring costs and the degree to which continuing external administration is required in running a camp.

Site Selection

A suitable site should be chosen as early as possible since that will influence all other decisions about layout and provision of services. The site should be well drained, not prone to seasonal flooding, landslide, tidal waves, or sea surges, and located as close as possible to a main road to ease supply problems. If international support is anticipated, a site with reasonable access to an airport or port should be selected. Locating a camp away from existing urban areas makes access easier and can minimize administrative problems, but for long-term resettlement a site close to an existing community facilitates the provision of transport and employment.

Around urban areas, where the pressure on land is high, camp land may be available precisely because it is unsuited to residential use. The possibility of acquiring land by purchase or from government holdings should be considered.

Camp Layouts

Permanent communities are characterized not only by their buildings and streets but also by their social cohesion. Since people share services and have common needs, they evolve mutual obligation systems which regulate behavior in regard to property protection, waste and water disposal, latrine use, and play areas for children. In shantytowns these mechanisms may be inadequate, but in camps they will be lacking entirely. Such lack of social cohesion contributes to the spread of disease (e.g., by failure to use latrines) and makes camp administration more difficult. Adequate and early attention to physical layout will minimize such problems.

Camps should ideally be laid out so that a small cluster of families is grouped around and thus within easy reach of communal services. Access to a set of services (latrines, a water point) should be limited to a fixed group of people, and individual ''communities'' within the camp small enough so that people can know and work with their neighbors. Many administrative tasks such as latrine maintenance and disease surveillance can be partially delegated to these groups instead of being assigned to an employed workforce. The camp can be expanded with no reduction in the quality of services by adding units at the periphery.

Grid layouts with square or rectangular housing areas intersected by parallel roads, which were widely used in the past, have the advantages of the ease with which water, drainage, and power systems can be incorporated in the camp plan and of a high population density where land is in short supply. The latter advantage may also be a disadvantage since it is likely to encourage the spread of disease. Grid camps are relatively unsuitable for family occupation and should be avoided, particularly for long-term use.

Camp Services

Water Supply

If the camp is close to a public water supply, a connection may be possible and an important problem solved. Other systems and sources such as self-contained pumps or purifiers may be used, but they are more costly and require regular maintenance. In some areas tube or dug wells may provide cheap drinking water of high quality.

Contamination of water in temporary storage facilities such as collapsible tanks or household containers is common. Adequate water chlorination and daily residual chlorine and bacteriologic monitoring will prevent sickness.

Excreta Disposal

At least one latrine should be provided for every 20 people, and latrines should be sited for easy access from any part of the camp to encourage their use.

Health Services

If the camp is well organized and has adequate sanitation, water, and food supply standards, health conditions will be like those in the general population. Unless there is clear medical justification, providing a higher standard of care to camp residents than to the general population should be avoided. Health services can be provided by assigning volunteers or government health workers to the camp or enlarging the capacity of the nearest fixed health facility.

Other required services such as solid waste disposal, washing facilities, recreation areas, and power are discussed in M. Assar, *A Guide to Sanitation in Natural Disasters* (Geneva, World Health Organization, 1971).

Chapter 8

COMMUNICATIONS AND TRANSPORT*

Effective management of health relief requires access to and control of adequate transport and communications. The health sector's resources are usually insufficient to meet those needs. The Health Relief Coordinator will therefore require extensive support from the public works ministry, armed forces, and sometimes private sector to carry out essential relief tasks.

Responsibility for all emergency government transport and communications should be centralized in a single office in the national emergency committee which can coordinate their use with defined relief needs (see Chapter 1).

Communications

Adequate telephone, teleprinter, and emergency radio facilities are necessary for maintaining contact with health facilities and relief personnel in the field and with governmental agencies and international organizations.

In most countries the government has allotted specific radio frequencies and equipment to the military, police, fire, ambulance, and other public agencies, which also have access to commercial teleprinter and telephone services that allow them to send messages internationally. Emergency communications are normally part of a disaster plan, but if not the Health Relief Coordinator will need to ensure continuous access to them.

Telephone Service

Even if telephone service is not damaged, lines will be jammed with unessential calls. Several measures may be used to alleviate this problem. Installation of additional lines will be necessary to ensure enough circuits for national and international calls, and it will be crucial to advise all concerned overseas governments and agencies of new numbers as soon as they are in operation. A separate number must be assigned to public queries to avoid confusion and tying up other lines. The public must be asked through the broadcast and print media not to use the telephone system for unessential calls. Finally, it is important for the Health Relief Coordinator to maintain a written log, however terse, of all telephone communications.

Teleprinter Service

Teleprinters should be used for international communication whenever possible. The written record they provide minimizes the possibility of misunderstanding. If

---

*The contributions of Mr. Milford R. Fink (communications), Chief, Emergency Communications, Disaster Services, American Red Cross, and Mr. Robert Walker (transport), Coordinator of Emergency Operations, UNICEF, were particularly valuable in the final preparation of this chapter.

they are not available in health offices, they may be found in the offices of multinational corporations, hotels, the Red Cross, or United Nations agencies. Predisaster planning will facilitate their availability during emergencies.

Amateur Radio Service (Hams)

Amateur radio operators are licensed by their governments in most countries and their networks can be of great value in emergency communications. After some disasters they have been the only link with the outside world. Although most amateur operators display a great sense of discipline and responsibility, the accuracy of their reports may vary greatly. Hams should therefore be warned through the local press, radio, and television that no independent statements should be broadcast and that they should stay off the air unless their services are needed as part of governmental or accredited relief agencies' communications. Unless these measures are strictly enforced, hams may add to the confusion. Amateur radio equipment provides short-, intermediate-, and long-range communication.

Citizens' Band Radio (CB)

This radio service has been established in most countries under government regulation and allows licensed persons and organizations to use short-range radio communications for their business or personal activities. CB licensees can provide emergency communications over one to 20 miles with their personally owned base and mobile stations. CB equipment must be operated under the control of a licensee at all times. Operators can be recruited and instructed in the same way as hams.

Donated Radio Transceivers

After a major disaster there may be an outpouring of assistance or donation offers from other countries, organizations, and businesses. Supplemental radio equipment is occasionally included in these offers, but often the radio units are delivered well after they are needed. To expedite purchase and shipment of radio units, it is necessary for the donor to be advised of the type of radio units required, authorized transmitting and receiving frequencies, output requirements (wattage), the number of units needed, and the type and number of antennas required.

Effective communication after disaster does not depend exclusively on the nature and quantity of equipment available but primarily on the willingness of authorities to exchange and communicate specific and detailed information to the public, other governmental agencies, and the international community.

Transport

Coordination of Transport Facilities

Decision-making authority over a country's transport facilities is usually vested in its leadership and often the military and police are involved. Health ministries will therefore have to coordinate their transportation and logistics requirements with such authorities.

In times of emergency it may be most effective to place all collective vehicles such as buses and trucks, fuel stocks, and large public or private automotive workshops under a central authority. Such an office will include representation from agencies other than the health ministry since, for example, the military is unlikely to relinquish control over any equipment it provides during relief operations. Nevertheless, the emergency transport office must retain the right to establish priorities for using transport and insure that its directives are followed. Thus health authorities should be able to ensist that transport be provided for a thorough survey of the disaster area and movement of medical personnel.

Requirements for Transport Equipment

Vehicles and other means of transport will be required to survey the disaster area, take health and supervisory personnel into the affected area, carry supplies and equipment to staging areas and into the disaster area, evacuate the sick and wounded, clear roads, remove bodies and animal carcasses, and ferry local and international media personnel and relief agency representatives to and from the affected area.

Inventory of Resources

As part of predisaster planning, an inventory should be made of vehicles in the country or province which can be commandeered for relief purposes after disasters. If not prepared in advance, a limited inventory must be made at the time of the emergency with emphasis on collective transport, four-wheel cars and trucks, and refrigerated vehicles. With some exceptions, vehicles donated from abroad arrive late—sometimes several weeks after the emergency.

Sources of Equipment

Figure 8 shows possible uses and sources of vehicles and logistics support equipment which may be available for use in the period immediately after a disaster. The uses suggested are flexible and depend on the actual situation (as with the use of boats in a flood), and potential sources will vary from country to country. It is often more realistic to rely on national rather than on international sources.

The disaster relief coordinator should also give forethought to the logistical support required to carry out a relief operation. These include fuels and lubricants, road-clearing and cargo-handling equipment, and trained drivers and vehicle mechanics. The mechanics are needed to ensure that the vehicles in emergency reserve are kept in operating condition.

Figure 8. Possible uses and sources of transport equipment available during immediate postdisaster period.

Vehicle type	USES													SOURCES					
	Survey of disaster area	Transport health personnel	Evacuation	Supplies to staging area	Supplies to/within affected area	Removal bodies	Removal/burial animal carcasses	Transport media personnel	Road clearing	Water supplies	Fuel supplies	Supply handling	Epidemiological surveillance	Functional ministries	Military	Local commercial dealers	Private/commercial ownership	Foreign agencies/governments	Red Cross other NGO's
Ambulance	✓	✓	✓											✓	✓			✓	✓
Utility 4-wheel drive (Land Rover or equival.)		✓	✓		✓	✓		✓		✓	✓		✓	✓	✓	✓	✓	✓	✓
Pickup truck		✓	✓		✓	✓	✓	✓		✓	✓		✓	✓	✓	✓	✓	✓	✓
Van/station wagon		✓	✓		✓	✓		✓					✓	✓	✓	✓	✓		✓
Motorcycles	✓	✓	✓					✓					✓	✓	✓	✓	✓		✓
Medium/heavy trucks					✓		✓	✓		✓	✓		✓	✓	✓	✓	✓		✓
Bicycles		✓			✓			✓					✓	✓		✓	✓		✓
Water tankers				✓	✓					✓				✓		✓	✓		
Boats (river)	✓	✓	✓	✓	✓	✓		✓							✓	✓	✓		✓
Barges (+ tugs)				✓	✓										✓	✓	✓		
Amphibious vehicles	✓	✓	✓		✓			✓							✓		✓	✓	
Helicopter	✓	✓	✓	✓	✓			✓			✓		✓		✓		✓	✓	
STOL aircraft	✓		✓	✓	✓			✓							✓		✓	✓	
Cargo aircraft			✓					✓							✓		✓	✓	
Amphibious aircraft	✓		✓		✓			✓							✓			✓	
Fuel tankers					✓						✓			✓	✓	✓	✓	✓	
Bulldozers							✓		✓					✓	✓		✓		
Auto cranes												✓			✓		✓		
Animal transport					✓	✓	✓	✓					✓			✓	✓		✓

51

Chapter 9

MANAGEMENT OF INTERNATIONAL
RELIEF ASSISTANCE

National self-reliance in disaster relief is a goal toward which all countries must strive, but international assistance may be needed to provide locally unavailable resources or skills for relief and rehabilitation. Many agencies, associations, groups, and governments aid countries affected by natural disasters. Each has different objectives, expertise, and financial support to offer, and over a hundred may become involved in any single major disaster. If properly coordinated, international relief is beneficial to disaster victims; if uncoordinated, its chaos and confusion will cause a "second disaster." A national government must be prepared in advance to assume its responsibility for coordination as it can hardly be improvised effectively after a disaster.

An essential step is to designate and train a senior health official to act as a focal point for emergency preparedness before the disaster and as coordinator afterward.

Agencies active in emergency relief fall into several categories—United Nations organizations, foreign governments, and nongovernmental organizations (see Annex 1).

United Nations Agencies

The United Nations Disaster Relief Office (UNDRO) is the agency responsible for mobilizing and coordinating international emergency relief resources. At the country level, the operational aspects of emergency relief are carried out by the local or regional office of the United Nations Development Program (UNDP). A request to UNDRO for assistance is regarded as a request for assistance from every United Nations agency. In health-related matters, UNDRO relies on the expertise of the World Health Organization (WHO) which, through its central (Geneva) or regional offices, can provide emergency technical cooperation (see Annex 1).

Government Agencies

Many governments provide assistance to countries after disasters, either on a government-to-government (bilateral) basis or through intergovernmental groups such as the Organization of American States (OAS) or European Economic Community (EEC). This assistance is usually given only after receipt of a specific request from the government of the affected country and is administered by a specific ministry or development agency.

Nongovernmental Organizations

Worldwide there are more than 400 nongovernmental agencies wholly or partly concerned with international disaster relief which provide material, expertise, or cash. Approximately 100 organizations belong to the International Council of Voluntary Agencies (ICVA), and the American Council of Voluntary Agencies for Foreign Service, an ICVA member which publishes the frequently updated *Directory of U.S. Non Profit Organizations in Development Assistance Abroad*, has 50 members in the United States. Many of these agencies are supported by contributions from the general public, although in some countries they also receive government funds. Voluntary agencies are often referred to by the telegraphic abbreviation "Volags" or, in United Nations parlance, "NGOs."

Nongovernmental organizations vary considerably in their approaches to disaster relief and the material contributions they can make.

Larger, experienced agencies and those already engaged in development work in the affected country tend to have a better understanding of the nature of the problems to be faced there. They engage in disaster relief only when there is an apparent need. Among the most experienced agencies, national Red Cross societies and the international League of Red Cross Societies in Geneva have been most active in disaster relief.

Agencies without prior commitment to the country concerned generally have less knowledge of local problems and sometimes harbor misconceptions about the needs created by a disaster. They can thus increase the pressure on the local government by demanding operational support (e.g., transport) that would be better allocated to another agency.

In addition, "ad hoc agencies"—those established, after by inexperienced persons, in response to a particular disaster—can be a major drain on the operational resources and patience of the government of an affected country. Some agencies of this type have made valuable contributions, however.

Obtaining International Disaster Relief

Most major agencies have disaster relief offices to which inquiries and requests for assistance should be directed. Suitable requests should be formulated as soon as possible after the disaster and directed to the appropriate agency. The appropriateness of an agency for meeting a specific request will depend on its resources, communications channels, and constraints.

Resources

Agencies can make cash grants, donate supplies, provide technical assistance, furnish food, or make loans. Some specialize in only one of these areas, while others have more general capabilities. An understanding of these resources is essential to avoid requesting cash from an agency that provides only assistance in kind or supplies from an agency that specializes in technical assistance.

Communications Channels

Communications channels are important because agencies may only accept requests for assistance from a specific source within the affected country and will only disseminate assistance through a specific agent or ministry there. For example, the

World Health Organization accepts requests for assistance only from health ministries and the League of Red Cross Societies distributes aid only through its national counterparts. Despite these channels, the health ministry, through the Health Relief Coordinator, is usually the final health authority in the affected country and must be informed of and control the type and quantity of health assistance arriving in the country.

Constraints

Agencies frequently operate within constitutional or statutory limits on their activities. Some require declaration of a state of emergency or a formal request from a government before they can respond. Most must account for their programs and expenditures to a supervisory political body or public overseers, thus making projects with high visibility and humanitarian appeal easier to fund than low-profile projects.

Agencies may also require first-hand or conclusive evidence of relief need to make expenditures or conduct fund raising, and so the health ministry should arrange visits to disaster areas for agency representatives.

Public pressure will also stimulate some foreign governments and agencies to commit funds or pledge support for specific projects or areas in the early stage of an emergency, sometimes a few days after the impact. The actual delivery of supplies or services may take considerably longer and before a thorough assessment of health sector priorities has been completed. The health sector must therefore prepare and submit preliminary cost estimates for relief and rehabilitation needs as soon as possible and before all funds available are exhausted.

A final constraint on some agencies is time, for their ability to respond to a request for assistance quickly varies greatly. Delays between identification of needs and actual assistance are thus unavoidable and sometimes prolonged. Future needs must therefore be anticipated, a task in which UNDRO and the World and Pan American Health Organizations can collaborated if necessary.

Coordinating International Disaster Relief

The affected country must make definite administrative arrangements to communicate with, coordinate, and supervise the work of governmental and nongovernmental organizations. This can be best accomplished in regular meetings of a committee headed by a national emergency committee member and consisting of a representative from each of the major agencies. In addition, the agencies should each have a permanent liaison with the national emergency committee, thus enabling them to present problems to it as they arise.

As noted in Chapter 6, the government ought to state clearly that emergency health supplies and personnel should not be sent unless specifically requested. This statement should be circulated to all potential suppliers of assistance and its diplomatic and consular representatives abroad.

Volunteers

Despite such a statement, the arrival of unsolicited medical assistance, particularly in the form of volunteer physicians, may be a persistent problem. On the one hand, self-supporting teams from neighboring countries or regions with the same culture and language provide valuable assistance. On the other, individual foreign volunteers unfamiliar with local conditions, unaffiliated with a recognized agency, and in some instances with unconfirmed academic credentials have been most counterproductive.

The simplest way of dealing with this problem may be for the affected country to deny admission to any medical volunteers who arrive without institutional accreditation and support. As a corollary, if foreign medical graduates and other health workers are allowed to work in the affected country after a disaster, provision will have to be made for their temporary registration or licensing requirements to be waived and for the provision or waiver of malpractice insurance if required.

Chapter 10

REESTABLISHING NORMAL PROGRAMS

In the first weeks after disaster the pattern of health needs will change rapidly, from casualty treatment toward more normal primary health care. Services must be reorganized, often because many permanent facilities have been severely damaged and severe financial constraints on reconstruction exist. Priorities will also shift from health care toward environmental health measures and temporary shelters.

The Health Relief Coordinator will be faced with decisions in three main areas which must not be overlooked during the emergency operations: the long-term problems caused by the disaster, reestablishing normal health services, and assessing and repairing or reconstructing damaged facilities and buildings.

Long-term Problems Caused by the Disaster

Extended Need for Medical Care

If large numbers of casualties have resulted from the disaster, a small proportion (probably less than 1 per cent) will require long-term nursing at home, institutional care, or specialized rehabilitation for months or years. Examples are paraplegics, patients with severe brain damage, amputees, and patients with chronic sepsis. In countries where specialized services for long-term care and rehabilitation are limited, this will put a strain on the health services.

Funding long-term programs from international resources may prove difficult since many organizations are reluctant to take on such expenditures. Preliminary statistics on the numbers of patients involved and estimates of cost should be obtained as soon as possible and made available to decision makers and interested agencies.

Surveillance of Communicable Diseases

As the weeks pass after a disaster, the public is likely to become progressively less concerned about the risk of epidemic diseases, even though outbreaks may still occur, and its initial enthusiasm for providing emergency services to temporary settlements may wane. Disease surveillance remains important and should be continued until normal disease reporting systems can be restored.

Care of Orphans

A major disaster with high mortality leaves orphaned children whose care may become the responsibility of health agencies. Institutional care should be a last resort because of its recurring cost, administrative difficulties, and the social harm to the orphans which may result. Each case should be reviewed separately to see if there are surviving relations who can undertake the child's care, and in most countries this is usually possible because of extended family networks. The Red Cross has considerable experience in tracing displaced children and can be asked for assistance. Offers from nongovernmental organizations to arrange rapid adoption abroad should be considered with greatest caution.

Reestablishing Normal Health Services

Two problems may occur in restoring predisaster health services. In some cases, resources budgeted for six months or a year are depleted in a few days of emergency relief operations, and in disasters attracting massive voluntary or foreign government aid, the emergency level of services or care may temporarily exceed what the country can customarily afford.

Since a sizable portion of the assistance in kind pledged immediately after the impact will continue to arrive in the disaster area for several weeks, the Health Relief Coordinator should keep in mind anticipated rehabilitation needs when formulating his original request. As noted earlier, the acceptance of some forms of assistance such as field hospitals or volunteers should also be decided on in light of longer-term needs.

The rehabilitation period provides an opportunity for making major changes in health-care methods, for during it people are receptive to new ideas. For instance, programs such as laboratory services, epidemiologic surveillance, oral rehydration of diarrhea patients, and expanded immunization have been strengthened as an indirect result of floods in the Americas.

Assessment, Repair, and Reconstruction of Damaged Facilities and Buildings

When water supply and sewage systems, hospitals, and other health facilities (including stores and administrative buildings) have been damaged, the engineering section must arrange for a thorough survey to supplement the preliminary assessment and provide detailed cost estimates.

If international assistance is required for reconstruction, the estimate can be used to draw up projects to obtain the necessary funding or loans. Project plans should be as accurate and detailed and be submitted as soon as possible after the disaster, since this will improve the likelihood of obtaining funds.

Chapter 11

DISASTER PREPAREDNESS

Few types of natural catastrophe can now be predicted accurately. Exceptions are tidal waves and to a lesser extent destructive winds. Although hurricanes can be tracked by weather satellites, their exact point of impact remains uncertain until very shortly before it occurs.

Earthquakes, destructive winds, and floods do occur in well-defined areas particularly prone to natural hazards, however. Preparedness for disaster is therefore possible.

Where disaster is a regular and recurrent threat, disaster planning is generally incorporated into the government structure. In countries where the risk of disaster is real but their occurrence infrequent, the difficulties and cost of maintaining a sophisticated preparedness structure must be recognized.

Disaster preparedness is a permanent multisectoral activity to which the health sector's contribution is essential. Disaster preparedness consists of:

Vulnerability Analysis

This is carried out mostly by other government agencies and the health sector's responsibility is usually limited to the vulnerability of health facilities, buildings, and services including water systems.

Establishment of a National Coordination Mechanism

This requires that special legislation be adopted and often that an office of civil defense be set up. A health official should be appointed the focal point for disaster preparedness and as Health Relief Coordinator in case of disasters (see Chapter 1).

Health legislation may have to be amended to provide extraordinary authority for waiving death certification and formalities, licensing foreign physicians and other health workers to practice legally in the country, waiving import regulations affecting key supplies such as certain drugs, and requisitioning private services or goods.

Preparation of Operation Plans

Predisaster planning does not consist of the one-time preparation of a plan but is a continuous process in all essential public sectors such as health, water, and power. The following guidelines should be kept in mind:

(1) Plan for probable events and likely health needs created by disaster (see Part I). To be effective, planning must be directed toward specific and realistic ends such as how to cope with unsolicited assistance and making the best use of available resources.

(2) Plan for the main features of administrative response such as the location and general responsibilities of key officials. Do not complicate plans with detail. Allow for ad hoc and improvised responses to fill in gaps.

(3) Subdivide plans into self-sufficient units. Adequate response to a disaster generally does not require specialized officials such as hospital administrators to know the entire plan.

(4) Disseminate the plan. To function properly, people with roles in it must know of the plan, which demands considerable training. Too many good plans have failed during emergencies for lack of adequate dissemination.

(5) Include exercises to test the plan periodically, for plans are not realistic if they are not exercised. The absence of actual testing will largely negate even the best of abstract plans.

It is essential to keep information updated constantly on the locations, names, telephone numbers, addresses, and duties of all key officials on the national emergency and health relief committees. Similar information must be maintained on the organizational structure and contact points of all key services in the health and related sectors. Examples are main disease control services; urban utilities including gas, water, sewage, and refuse disposal; hospitals and clinics; private health facilities; drug companies and stores; police and military forces; and United Nations and major international agencies (see Annex 1).

The functions and respective responsibilities of civil defense, military, and police in regard to health and a hierarchy for controlling individual units must be defined. Often the national emergency or civil defense committee will have final authority. The relationship between civilian and military personnel and resources should be decided and specific provision made for the use of military services such as helicopters for surveying and assessment.

Hospitals

In areas prone to earthquake and destructive winds, each hospital should have a disaster plan designed to cope with a sudden influx of casualties. A hospital's plan should take into account the possibility of severe damage to its structure and service utilities. Hospital disaster planning has four main components: patient and staff safety in case of disaster; management of mass casualties; staff alert, recall, and deployment; and operations control including information and communications. Fuller information on this subject will be found in P. E. Savage, *Disasters and Hospital Planning: A Manual for Doctors, Nurses and Administrators* (Oxford, Pergamon Press, 1979).

Stockpiling

In areas where disaster is infrequent and health budgets are small, it is uneconomic to stockpile disaster relief supplies. The expenses of storing and turning over stocks to maintain quality add substantially to the cost of the supplies themselves. Several alternatives exist: normal operating stocks in health facilities and government warehouses may be expanded to cover immediate emergency needs; countries with similar disaster potentials can develop regional stockpiles from which deliveries can be made quickly because distances within the region are short; and military stockpiles can be used since they often include drugs and equipment suitable for emergency health use.

Background Data and Inventory of Resources

Assessment of needs and interpretation of data after the impact and, in general, good management of relief operations requires access to background information on the incidence of relevant communicable diseases; nutritional status; marketing facilities and places of bulk food storage; methods of and geographic variations in water supply and sanitation; vector control and immunization programs; and possible sources of specialized assistance in nutrition, epidemiology, and other technical fields.

Topographic maps showing roads, bridges, railways, and health facilities, and demographic maps indicating rough variations in total and relative density, major economic and ethnic areas, and places subject to natural catastrophes such as floods are often hard to locate in the aftermath of a disaster and should be procured and stored accessibly in advance.

A detailed inventory of all material resources is unrealistic and unnecessary. A directory of knowledgeable sources of information or supplies will generally be sufficient.

Training of Health Personnel and the Public

Satisfactory preparedness cannot be achieved solely by drawing up operational plans, stockpiling supplies, and compiling information. Health ministries in countries vulnerable to disaster should consider a comprehensive training program. Specific training in first aid, search and rescue techniques, and public hygiene should be given to the population at risk, and health officials should be instructed continuously in their respective areas of responsibility.

Part III
ANNEXES

Annex 1

EXTERNAL AGENCIES PROVIDING HEALTH RELIEF

Every country is a potential source of health relief for some other disaster-stricken nation. Bilateral assistance, whether in personnel, supplies, or cash, is probably the most important source of external aid. Several intergovernmental or regional agencies have established special funds, procedures and offices to provide emergency assistance.

This annex uses selected examples to illustrate the broad variety of extranational agencies that provide health assistance after natural disasters. Because the list is short, not all experienced and dedicated agencies providing valuable emergency assistance are included in it.

United Nations Agencies

United Nations Disaster Relief Office (UNDRO)

On 14 December 1971, the United Nations General Assembly established the Office of the United Nations Disaster Relief Coordinator.

UNDRO's responsibilities after disaster are, as set out in the Resolution, to: (1) furnish precise information as to relief requirements; (2) mobilize and coordinate disaster relief from United Nations agencies and the international community in general in response to a request for assistance from the stricken state; (3) maintain a clearing house in Geneva to exchange information and match needs with supplies and services from donor sources; and (4) make advance arrangements for emergency assistance which donor countries and organizations are prepared to furnish.

By agreement with UNDRO, United Nations Development Program (UNDP) Resident Representatives also represent UNDRO in individual countries. They provide a channel for requests from governments in all disaster-related matters. When a disaster strikes and with assistance as necessary from staff dispatched by UNDRO, they lead the United Nations team in assessing emergency needs and locally coordinating aid from the United Nations system and other international sources. UNDP can also furnish some financial aid in emergencies and, if necessary, adapt its country development programs to rehabilitation and reconstruction needs.

World Health Organization (WHO)

WHO is responsible for coordinating international health action. The Pan American Health Organization (PAHO) and other WHO regional offices act as focal points for national health authorities and donors after disasters in their respective areas.

WHO can provide technical cooperation in assessing health-related needs, coordinating international health assistance, inventorying health relief supplies, carrying out epidemiologic surveillance and disease control measures, assessing environmental health, managing health services, formulating cost estimates and relief projects, and procuring relief supplies.

WHO and its regional offices can provide limited material assistance by reprogramming country development activities or from other sources.

United Nations Children's Fund (UNICEF)

UNICEF assists programs in most developing countries for the health, education, and welfare of children and mothers. These activities employ materials that can usefully be diverted to meet emergencies in disaster areas or can be drawn from an emergency stockpile in the UNICEF warehouse at Copenhagen. The Executive Director of UNICEF has a substantial cash reserve at his disposal for rapid use in emergencies and can divert funds from regular programs to emergency operations with the agreement of the government concerned. In consequence, though UNICEF's main interest after a disaster is the medium-term restoration and long-term development of services to children and mothers, it is geared to provide substantial emergency assistance for those vulnerable groups. It can also procure relief supplies on behalf of UNDRO, other United Nations agencies, and other relief organizations. UNICEF coordinates its health activities closely with WHO.

World Food Program (WFP)

WFP furnishes large amounts of foodstuffs in support of economic and social development projects in developing countries. In addition, it has substantial resources with which to meet emergency food needs, some of which can often be furnished from project food stocks already in a disaster-stricken country. WFP also purchases and ships food needed in emergencies on behalf of donor governments, UNDRO, or stricken countries themselves, and its field staff can help coordinate the receipt and use of food aid from all sources. WFP cooperates closely with WHO in the nutritional monitoring of emergencies.

Food and Agriculture Organization (FAO)

FAO provides technical cooperation and promotes investment in long-term agricultural development. It also tries to prevent food shortages in the event of widespread crop failures or disasters. The Director General has at his disposal a ready source of food aid in the commodities pledged to WFP for his use in emergencies. In both relief and short-term rehabilitation operations, FAO specialists help assess needs in the agricultural and food sectors and prevent animal diseases.

Intergovernmental Organizations

Organization of American States (OAS)

OAS operates the Inter-American Fund for Assistance in Emergency Situations (FONDEM), which is administered by a committee of representatives from OAS, the Inter-American Development Bank, and PAHO. Subject to the availability of voluntarily contributed funds, FONDEM provides food, medical supplies, and other relief to member states affected by disaster.

European Economic Community (EEC)

EEC has set aside more than $280 million for emergency aid over five years for the African-Caribbean-Pacific (ACP) countries that signed the Lomé II Convention in 1980. Sixty million dollars from the Community's general budget were allocated in 1979 for disaster relief in other countries. EEC assistance is divided into (1) life-saving assistance to be used shortly after the signing of financing agreements for relief goods such as medical supplies, water treatment equipment, tents, blankets, or food bought locally or from EEC countries; (2)

rehabilitation funds, mostly to restore social and economic activities to normal by providing such things as insecticides, fertilizers, fuel, and vehicles and spare parts; and (3) in addition, emergency food aid in the form of cereals, milk powder, and butter oil which can be donated to populations affected by disasters.

Nongovernmental Organizations

League of Red Cross Societies

The League, headquartered in Geneva, is a world federation of 126 national Red Cross, Red Crescent, and Red Lion and Sun societies. It coordinates relief operations internationally and operates within an affected country through the member national society or its own staff if no local society exists. The League obtains cash donations and specific emergency items through international appeals and donates them through the national society.

Assistance provided by the League or national societies consists of food, shelter, medical supplies, volunteer workers, and in some cases self-supporting field hospitals and medical teams. Its long experience and considerable flexibility and resources make it a most valuable nongovernmental source of support and cooperation with the health sector.

International Committee of the Red Cross (ICRC)

ICRC is a private and strictly neutral Swiss organization whose basic concern is people affected by war and civil conflicts. If a natural disaster should befall war refugees, for example, ICRC can provide aid in kind and services, particularly nutritional and medical assistance.

CARE (Cooperative for American Relief Everywhere)

CARE, whose headquarters is in New York, provides emergency relief in the form of food, hand tools, and similar goods to disaster-affected communities. Its postdisaster projects include rehabilitation of water supply systems, rebuilding houses, and provision of basic sanitary or health facilities. MEDICO, an affiliate, maintains health-care and training teams in 10 countries. CARE's policy is to cooperate closely with and respond to requests from government authorities.

CARITAS International

This organization, more formally known as the International Confederation of Catholic Charities, is a federation of national CARITAS organizations in 91 countries. CARITAS International stimulates, coordinates, and supports the relief activities of its member societies.

Catholic Relief Services (CRS)

CRS, an American organization, responds rapidly to emergencies by providing food, clothing, medical supplies, and shelter. Assistance is coordinated with the national CARITAS organization and the local Catholic clergy. CRS employs health professionals such as public health advisers and nutritionists who work closely with national health authorities.

Lutheran World Relief Federation (LWR)

LWR represents Lutheran churches of various denominations in the United States. It can provide assistance in kind following disasters as well as loans for longer-term reconstruction.

Mennonite Central Committee

This organization represents Mennonite churches in the United States and provides technical assistance and financial support for specific community projects.

OXFAM

OXFAM is an international relief organization with affiliated autonomous agencies in Australia, Belgium, Canada, Great Britain, and the United States. It has developed considerable expertise in managing refugee camps, nutritional relief, and housing projects. OXFAM/England has designed an emergency sanitation system for use in camps. Immediate relief aid is one of OXFAM's top priorities.

International Salvation Army

The International Salvation Army, headquarted in London, and its national affiliates can provide health-care assistance and supplies of various kinds.

Save the Children Fund/Federation

The Fund (in the United Kingdom), Federation (in the United States), and sister agencies assist in community nutrition and water treatment projects.

Seventh-Day Adventist World Services (SAWS)

SAWS, headquartered in Washington, specializes in health programs such as hospitals, dispensaries, and child feeding. It employs a considerable number of physicians, dentists, and nurses overseas.

World Council of Churches

The Council is a fellowship of more than 270 Protestant and Orthodox denominations around the world whose headquarters is in Geneva. Through its member churches, it provides various kinds of health assistance after disasters. Church World Services, a component, is the disaster relief agency of 30 Protestant and Orthodox churches in the United States and can provide a broad range of support to health projects. Christian Action for Development in the Caribbean (CADEC), a subgroup of the Caribbean Council of Churches, operates a disaster office responsible for coordinating disaster relief in the Caribbean.

Additional information on the various nongovernmental organizations and voluntary agencies active in relief activities can be obtained from:

The International Council of Voluntary Agencies
17, Avenue de la Paix
CH 1202 Geneva, Switzerland

or

The American Council of Voluntary Agencies for Foreign Service
Technical Assistance Information Clearing House (TAICH)
200 Park Avenue South
New York, New York 10003
USA

Annex 2

BIBLIOGRAPHY

Ahearn, F., and B. R. Castellón. Problemas de salud mental después de una situación de desastre. *Boletín de la Oficina Sanitaria Panamericana* 85(1):1-15 (1978).

Berenson, A. S. (ed.) *Control of Communicable Diseases in Man.* 12th ed. Washington, American Public Health Association, 1980.

de Ville de Goyet, C., et al. Earthquake in Guatemala: epidemiologic evaluation of the relief effort. *Bulletin of the Pan American Health Organization* 10(2):95-109 (1976).

Glass, R. I., et al. Earthquake injuries related to housing in a Guatemalan village. *Science* 197:638-43 (1977).

Gurd, C. H., et al. The health management of Cyclone Tracy. *Medical Journal of Australia* 1:641-44 (1975).

Mason, J., and P. Cavalié. Malaria epidemic in Haiti following a hurricane. *American Journal of Tropical Medicine and Hygiene* 4(4):1-10 (1965).

Manning, D. *Disaster Technology: An Annotated Bibliography.* Oxford, Pergamon Press, 1975.

Romero, A., et al. Some epidemiologic features of disasters in Guatemala. *Disasters* 2:39-46 (1978).

Savage, P. E. *Disasters and Hospital Planning: A Manual for Doctors, Nurses and Administrators.* Oxford, Pergamon Press, 1979.

Somner, A., and W. H. Mosley. West Bengal cyclone of November 1970. *Lancet* I:1029-36 (1972).

The Treatment and Prevention of Diarrhoeal Disease. Geneva, World Health Organization, 1976.

Western, K. *The Epidemiology of Natural and Man-Made Disasters; the Present State of the Art.* Dissertation for the Academic Diploma in Tropical Public Health, London School of Hygiene and Tropical Medicine, University of London (1972).

Whittaker, R., et al. Earthquake disaster in Nicaragua: reflections on the initial management of massive casualties. *Journal of Trauma* 14(1):37-43 (1974).